*

IMPERSONAL PASSION

*

*

DENISE RILEY

* IMPERSONAL PASSION *

LANGUAGE AS AFFECT

*

DUKE UNIVERSITY PRESS

Durham and London 2005

*

*

An earlier version of "Malediction"

was published as "Bad Words" in

Diacritics 31, no. 4 (2001), copyright Johns

Hopkins University. A version of "What I

Want Back Is What I Was" was published in

Diacritics 32, no. 1 (2002), copyright

Johns Hopkins University. "The Right

to Be Lonely" was first published in

differences 13, no. 1 (spring 2002),

copyright Brown University

and *differences*.

CONTENTS

ACKNOWLEDGMENTS

Several friends, colleagues, and students patiently put up with a small bombardment of at least a couple of these essays in draft. For their suggestions and their time, I'm grateful to Amanda Bay, Emma Bell, Jon Cook, Mladen Dolar, Spyridon Georgias, Annie Janowitz, Jean-Jacques Lecercle, Colin MacCabe, Angela McRobbie, Andrew Sola, Barbara Taylor, and Alenka Zupancic.

For their faithfully incisive readings of the whole lot, I'm (as ever) deeply indebted to Judith Butler and to Joan Scott. I owe special thanks to Wendy Brown and to Ellen Rooney.

One or two of the essays were aired at the Institute for the Humanities at the University of Michigan in 2004; I thank my fellow Fellows for their observations, and the Institute's Director, Daniel Herwitz. Helpful comments at the last minute were offered by members of the Aesthetics seminar in the University of Michigan's philosophy department, and by those who kindly heard me out at the Department of Rhetoric at the University of California, Berkeley.

This writing was completed thanks only to a study leave from the School of English and American Studies at the University of East Anglia in 2002, and to a successive term of research leave funded by the Arts and Humanities Research Board in 2003: I am most grateful to these bodies for their support.

I thank Courtney Berger and Kate Lothman at Duke University Press for their editorial help.

An earlier version of "Malediction" appeared as "Bad Words" in Dia-

tale of what he called "word attacks": spasmodically violent and unwilled upsurges of one of his earlier and preferred languages. His agon of words needn't be held to occur so "independently" of what the words signified; this would be his argument. It's also, of course, an antique ground of debate. Yet if, for example, it's intuitively evident that tension, unease, or a feeling of dispossession can result from the gulf between the ostensible content of what's said, and the affect which seeps from the very form of the words—in short, unexamined rhetoricity is at stake—we still seem not to own much of a descriptive vocabulary to characterize this relative autonomy of language, or have let slip what vocabulary there once was. It's not just a matter of the unspoken "implications" of what's said, but something stronger: of how language as the voice of its occasion can also inflect its speakers. And the difficulty persists of naming this aspect of the life of language, if it's no longer held to be hard bound in the narrows of semantic meaning, nor, as a reaction, abandoned to babbling frilliness.

This descriptive difficulty, though, has many fine resources at its disposal; speculation here can draw on a broadly scattered but richly venerable literature which, ripe with impassioned linguistic disagreement and tortured by political and philosophical fashion, has for centuries done battle with the speaking of language itself. Here the provocations issued by the dead include the gallery of the ancients, such as Aristotle, Longinus, and Quintilian. From the more recent dead have come, for instance, Marx's elegantly dramatic history of repetition's dethroning powers and the comedy of slogans, James's neat observation "We ought to say a feeling of *and*, a feeling of *if*, a feeling of *but*, and a feeling of *by*, quite as readily as we say a feeling of blue or a feeling of cold"; Kleist's persuasion of the understanding which, beginning in blindness, builds itself up through voiced exchange; Nietzsche's furious alertness to the bossy dictates of grammar and its supposed wiles; Freud's scrutiny of the joke as the word which plays the speaker, or the pathologies of plaintive reiteration; Bakhtin's early invocation of lyric shame, or Benjamin's luminous polemic about language as exiled; Jakobson's fascination with those poetic intricacies which outpace their authors' intentions; Heidegger's demonstrations, insistently painstaking, built up in layers like a kind of tiling, that we dwell in the house of language;

Adorno's dedication to the strain between the "poetic" and the "conceptual"; Empson's fecund and proliferating ambiguities; Wittgenstein's conviction that linguistic experience is, after all, as much an experience as any other kind; Lacan's focus on the compulsions of the long chains of a discourse which "reproduces a small circuit in which an entire family, an entire coterie, an entire camp, an entire nation or half the world will be caught"; Foucault's captivation by the thought of the outside, that far side of language onto which any speaker's slightness can vertiginously open out; Althusser's naming of a strange temporality of the guilt lodged at the core of identification's imperatives; Beckett's late monologues as a stoical embodiment of sheer utterance set against pathos; Merleau-Ponty's insistence that thought only receives its being through articulation, so that "the most familiar thing appears indeterminate as long as we have not recalled its name"; Barthes's isolation of the singing of the voice as a limb; Forrest-Thomson's precise delineation of poetry's true artifice; Deleuze's and Guattari's fingering of words' organizing violence; Williams's thought of the emergence of a forceful style of language which runs well ahead of its codified recognition; Oliver's calibrations of poetry's voiced emotionality; and Volosinov's delineation of the exteriority of inner speech and the interpenetration of the psychic and the linguistic, taut notes whose lucidity remains breathtaking.[2]

My transparently selective list of the dead, rustling with its omissions, is intended only to gesture toward a great range of conceptual writings about language at work, all of them reflections which don't set what Canetti called the agon of words against meaning. Descending abruptly from their heights, the following essays are pragmatic, their emphasis not so much on How to Do Things with Words, as Austin's title had it, but How Words Do Things with Us.[3] And that "with us"—as distinct from "to us"—is pivotal. If language exerts a torsion on its users, it does not immobilize them, let alone strangle them. Quite why it doesn't, and how, is a main preoccupation of these essays. They listen to common twists of speech which in themselves enact feeling, rather than simply and obediently conveying it as we elect. And so they fray at the edges of that usual antithesis (crudely, in "continental" versus analytic philosophy) between language as speaking us, and our status as freely choosing users of language. As a result they'll come closer to apprehending language's affect as that outward unconscious which hovers between people, rather than swimming upward from the privacy of each heart.

Laments, rhetorical questions, exonerations, comedies of verbal inhibition, and clichés (a cliché is not to be despised: its automatic comfort is the happy exteriority of a shared language which knows itself perfectly well to be a contentless but sociable turning outward toward the world) — these all exert themselves as ordinary effects which are, though, no mere embellishments or overtones on top of their speakers' intentions: they can even outrun them. Or they can make their speaker's sentiments virtually irrelevant. For instance, the capacity to forgive needs first to hear an apology. That alone may not be enough, but it is necessary; in the absence of such a declaration, forgiveness is impossible except from the impossibly angelic. An apology is a linguistic formula. To "say the words" or hear them said: *that* is what matters, first of all. Their sincerity is less crucial, is something to debate after the recital. But without that act, whether the feeling behind the verbal gesture is secretly hollow or not, all is lost. Indeed, only a slight amplification of the notion of the performative (an utterance which in itself brings about something by virtue of being voiced in the apt situation, like the "I do" in a marriage ceremony) would let us think of language as a performer in a scenario which grants the importance of sheer timing, of occasion, of the subjugation of the speaker to the situation, bearing in mind that subjugation (as, we must hope, at the wedding) needn't always be unhappy. As an example of this kind of extended performative, irony can expose the verbal and historically volatile nature of political formulations and slogans. This is why it brightens things up, and is energizing; it gives you a sense of history as not rigid, in that the word as such, if reiterated enough, can rise prominently upward to attract your scrutiny and indeed collapse into idiocy.[4] This is the lighter side of repetition; the heavier is the stuff of unhappy obsessive reiteration. There is also a dark quotidian poetics of ordinary language–saturated scenarios which from the onset exert their verbal violence, and entice to submission or shame.

These essays touch on some ordinarily incisive linguistic forces: the nervous questioning of inflated demands for explanation which spring from a dread of contingency, such as the longing to see the significantly personal in the face of accident ("Some WHYs and *why mes*"); the sensation of a distinctly linguistic embarrassment which in itself adds another layer of mortification ("All Mouth and No Trousers"); the ruthlessness of verbal haunting by the intractable authority of angry calling, the indwelling of hostile words ("Malediction"); the persistent feeling of lying when you're in fact truth telling, due not to a psychology of guilt but to the formulaic social excuse which overwhelms any truth content (" 'Lying' When You Aren't"); a defense of solitude in the teeth of the linguistic imperative to social inclusion ("The Right to Be Lonely"); the real impersonality and peculiar alienation of the supposed intimacy of one's own first name ("Your Name Which Isn't Yours"); the defensible verbal sheepishness which delays urgent announcements ("Linguistic Inhibition as a Cause of Pregnancy"); the apparently innocent inquiry which deftly hamstrings its addressee, or the disabling appeal of a "you lot want me dead" of a particular antiabortion rhetoric ("But Then I Wouldn't Be Here"); the false consolation of retrospect through which we tacitly allow ourselves to have been what in fact we never were ("What I Want Back Is What I Was").

This litany does sound somewhat emotionally overwrought. Aren't we talking about hypersensitivity here? Yet the conception of an affect-soaked power of language itself can be demonstrated quite pragmatically. If the affective quality of music can be granted to exist irrespective of its hearers' sensibilities and their quirks, then why not accord a similar relative independence to language's emotionality? There is a tangible affect in language which stands somewhat apart from the expressive intentions of an individual speaker; so language can work outside of its official content. This speaking of language is far more than its resonances, its timbre, its insinuations, its persuasive cadences, or its spontaneous wit. It can kill. The magical thought of linguistic voodoo has been recorded to work. I will die simply because the death sentence through the bone of sorcery was pointed at me; named as the one due to die, I will wither away. Here my belief is necessary, but what I believe is the animated word's power. So does this entire train of thought lead to a fatalistic idea of our determination by language? On the contrary, these essays hint that while in our ordinary speaking there are compelled and echoic elements, we get along—not despite, but with and through them. So there's no need to suppose that to reflect on language's workings in us must conjure a great and reified Language which speaks us so that we fall into quivering helplessness before it. Nor need language suffer a theatrical personification as a seducer glittering with ruses to entice the innocent. To consider language itself shouldn't plunge us into anxiety over a loss of our own "agency"; if anything, it makes helpfully complex this supposed agency in drawing it away from an imagined lonely (and dubious) mastery on the part of speakers. Nor is it a "reification of language" to consider its effects of torsion. On the contrary, the truer reification would be always to conceive of language as our tool. This stance that insists on language as an instrument of willed control glosses over its directing rawness.

But if there is to be some practical use for such musings, where might the political make itself felt in language's speaking? It bites at the level of identification, self-description, and other impacted linguistic-emotional rhetorical forms which would, if unexamined, remain obscured by the thick curtain of the term *ideology*. For instance, proliferating self-descriptions, as encouraged by a present historical moment of petrification in the "politics of the personal," only accumulate yet more candidates for embalming in the Museum of Me. This is the sort of practical difficulty which shadows those altering versions of the self pronounced by new kinds of identification which aim to liberalize yet which can paralyze. Political upheavals have turned on how, at critical points, people have become willing to understand themselves; here language is profoundly historical. But it's a history also riddled with its own amnesia, torpor, or calcification, as the residues of thought have thickened. A disquieting linguistic malaise can make itself sharply felt in periods of change when self-description becomes an acute witness to the disquiet of people conscious of an unease between outer definition and private demurring; an unease comprehensible through the observation that the business of being named and taking on a social category both come "from outside"; both are externally given, at the heart of a supposed inwardness. The outwardly given received idea first has to be made mine, to be interiorized as if I had summoned it up as my own creation, in order for it to live. It's through the ventriloquy of inner speech that this happens.[5]

Then if there's a saying of language itself, the accompanying burden of these essays is the impersonality of language—which nevertheless has its life as internally as any other human tissue. Yet I'll suggest that if in language's devices there's a necessary impersonality or alienation, those terms could be taken in a tranquil manner. While the very idea of an affect of language does suggest that the self stands at a certain remove from itself, this is well removed from a mournful rendering of the self as a dispossessed phenomenon in its own eyes. Language as a speaking thing, neither my master nor my instrument, is amiably indifferent to me. This isn't a heartless stance. It's arguably that coincidence of a vacant formula (as in "I love you") with the absolute plenitude of the speaker's emotion which is sublime.

These essays, though, try to avoid drawing too heavy a line between the apparent froth of the everyday and the graver tone of the political, since in practice the same inflections run straight through both registers with scant regard for their official relative weightings. Nor, in dwelling on the affective regularities of words themselves, have I intended to evoke any abstraction of a language floating like a tremulous veil above the rough surfaces of lived being. Instead I've preferred an older sense of language as robust, and fat with history.

ONE

Malediction

*

The worst words revivify themselves within us, vampirically. Injurious speech echoes relentlessly, years after the occasion of its utterance, in the mind of the one at whom it was aimed: the bad word, splinterlike, pierces to lodge. In its violently emotional materiality, the word is indeed made flesh and dwells amongst us—often long outstaying its welcome. Old word-scars embody a "knowing it by heart," as if phrases had been hurled like darts into that thickly pulsating organ. But their resonances are not amorous. Where amnesia would help us, we can't forget.

This sonorous and indwelling aspect of vindictive words might help to characterize how, say, racist speech works on and in its targets. But wouldn't such a speculation risk simply advocating a systematic cultivation of deafness on the part of those liable to get hurt—or worse, be a criticism of their linguistic vulnerability; "They just shouldn't be so linguistically sensitive"? There's much to be said, certainly, in favor of studiously practicing indifference. But the old playground chant of "sticks and stones may break my bones, but words can never hurt me" was always notoriously untrue. The success of a tactics of indifference to harsh speech will also depend on the vicissitudes of those words' fate in the world, and that lies beyond my control. I change too. The thing upon which malevolent accusation falls, I am still malleable, while the words themselves will undergo their own alterations in time, and so their import for me will weaken or intensify accordingly. On occasion the impact of violent speech may even be recuperable through its own incantation; the repetition of abusive language may be occasionally saved through the irony of iteration, which may drain the venom out of the original insult, and neutralize it by displaying its idiocy.[1] Yet angry interpellation's very failure to always work as intended (since at particular historical moments, I may be able to parody, to weaken by adopting, to corrode its aim) is also exactly what, at other times, works for it. In any event, interpellation operates with a deep indifference as to where the side of the good may lie. And we can't realistically build an optimistic theory of the eventual recuperability of linguistic harm. For here there's no guaranteed rational progress—nor, though, any inescapable irrationality. Repetition will breed its own confident mishearing,[2] but its volatile alterations lean neither toward automatic amelioration nor inevitable worsening.

This observation, though, leaves us with the still largely uninvestigated forensics of spoken injury. Pragmatic studies of swearing certainly exist, but swear words as such are not the topic I have in mind. Nor is "righteous" anger. My preoccupation here is far darker, and restricted to the extreme: some sustained hostility of unremitting verbal violence, like the linguistic voodoo which can induce the fading away of its target, a phenomenon which can't be dismissed as an archaism. The curse does work. Verbal attacks, in the moment they happen, resemble stoning. Then isn't it too labored to ask how they do damage: isn't the answer plain, that they hurt just as stones hurt? At the instant of their impact, so they do. Yet the peculiarity of violent words, as distinct from lumps of rock, is their power to resonate within their target for decades after the occasion on which they were weapons. Perhaps an urge to privacy about being so maliciously named may perpetuate the words' remorseless afterlife: I keep what I was told I was to myself, out of reserve, shame, a wish not to seem mawkish and other not-too-creditable reasons; yet even if I manage to relinquish my fatal stance of nursing my injury, it may well refuse to let go of me. Why, though, should even the most irrational of verbal onslaughts lodge in us as if it were the voice of justice; and why should it stubbornly resist ejection, and defy its own fading? For an accusation to inhere, must its human target already be burdened with her own prehistory of vulnerability, her psychic susceptibility; must it even depend on her anticipating readiness to accept, even embrace, the accusation that also horrifies her? Maybe, then, there's some fatal attraction from the aggression uttered in the present toward earlier-established reverberations within us—so that to grasp its lure, we would have to leave a linguistic account to turn instead to a prelinguistic psychic account. Yet here the standard contrast between the linguistic and the psychic, in which we are usually forced to plump for either the unconscious or language, is especially unhelpful. There's nothing beyond interpellation, if by that *beyond* is meant a plunge into an ether of the psyche as soon as we topple off the ledge of the historical and linguistic. For refusing these thoroughly synthetic alternatives needn't commit us to a belief in an instantaneous, ahistorical impact of the bad word—or to assume some primal word of injury which laid us open subsequently to verbal assault, as if the chronology of harm must always unfold in a straight line of descent.

The impact of violence in the present may indeed revive far older associations in its target. An accusation will always fall onto some kind of linguistic soil, be it fertile or poor; and here a well-prepared loam is no doubt commoner than a thin veneer on bare rock. Should we, though, necessarily call such a variation in anger's reception its "psychic" dimension, in a tone which implies a clear separation from the domain of words? There has, undoubtedly, to be something very strong at work to explain why we can't readily shake off some outworn verbal injury. The nature of this strong thing, though, might better be envisaged as a seepage or bleeding between the usual categorizations; it need not be allocated wholesale to an unconscious considered as lying beyond the verbal, or else to a sphere of language considered as narrowly functional.[3] For the deepest intimacy joins the supposedly linguistic to the supposedly psychic; these realms, distinct by discursive convention, are scarcely separable. Then instead of this distinction, an idea of affective words as they indwell might be more useful—and this is a broadly linguistic conception not contrasted to, or opposed to, the psychic. So, for instance, my amateur philology may be a quiet vengeance: my fury may be, precisely, an intense, untiring, scrupulous contemplation of those old words of malediction which have stuck under the skin.

The tendency of malignant speech is to ingrow like a toenail, embedding itself in its hearer until it's no longer felt to come "from the outside." The significance of its original emanation from another's hostility becomes lost to the recipient as a tinnitus of remembered attack buzzes in her inner ear.[4] The hard word reverberates—so much so that it holds the appeal of false etymology (it's easy to assume that *to reverberate* derives from characteristically self-repeating verbal actions, whereas it meant striking or beating back). That it reverberates, rather than echoes, places it well beyond the possibilities of ironic recuperation that Echo offers; reverberation will only resound, to its own limit. And rancorous phrases, matted in a wordy undergrowth, appear to be "on the inside" as one fights them down while they perpetually spring up again. This is where it's crucial to recall that the accusations originally came from the outside, and the rage they echo was another's rage. But this half-consolation of the realist's recourse to history is not enough. We also need to dedramatize the words as they continue their whirring, and to sedate their bitter resonances in the inner ear's present time. For however does anyone withstand this common experience of being etched and scored with harsh names? One art of survival, I'll suggest, is to concede that "yes, this person really wanted me dead then"; yet in the same breath to see that the hostile wish is not identical with the excessive hostility of the lingering word, which has its own slow-burning temporality. The accuser's personal rage has a different duration from the resonances of the recalled inner word: to be able to separate and apportion these two will help. We'd need to try out some art of seeing the denouncer as separate from the denunciation, while also at its mercy himself. Is there some stoical language practice to counter the property of accusation to continue its corrosive work, even though the accuser may have died years ago? How this might be attempted is ventured in the following discussion, where no kindly strategy of humanizing and forgiving the pronouncer of the bad word or of grasping the special susceptibility of its human target is suggested, but a cooler tactic of enhancing the objectification of the word itself. It's the very thinglike nature of the bad word which may, in fact, enable its target to find release from its insistent reverb.

Accusation Often Lodges in the Accused

There was until recently in Paris, on rue Pavée in the quatrième, a decrepit-looking language school which displayed in its window, in

English (on a dusty cloth banner, in fifties-style white on red lettering) this injunction: "Don't let the English language beat you—Master it before it masters you." A curious exhortation to have been chosen as a motto by any language school—since for the native speaker the onrush of language is unstoppable, yet the exhortation is also irrelevant for the nonnative, who's never subject to joyous capture by a language not her first.

But what certainly threatens any comforting notion of our mastering language is the gripping power of predatory speech, which needs our best defensive efforts in the face of its threatened mastery of us. It's true enough, though, that not only imperious accusation is apt to indwell. So can lyric, gorgeous fragments, psalms and hymns; beautiful speech also comes to settle in its listeners. There's an unholy coincidence between beauty and cruelty in their verbal mannerisms; citation, reiteration, echo, quotation may work benignly, or as a poetics of abusive diction. If graceful speech is memorable, by what devices do violently ugly and lovely language both inhere; what does the internal strumming of metrical quotation have in common with the compulsions of aggressive speech? Yet perhaps the happily resonant indwelling of lyric may be explained in ways also fitting the unhappy experience of being mastered by hard words far better forgotten. Evidently there exists what we could call "linguistic love," a love sparked and sustained by the appeal of another's spoken or written words—that is, by something in the loved person which is also not of her and which lies largely beyond her control—her language. But if there is a linguistic love which is drawn outward to listen, there's also linguistic hatred, felt by its object as drawn inward. A kind of "extimacy" prevails in both cases. Imagined speech hollows can resemble a linguistic nursing home, in which old fragments of once-voiced accusation or endearment may resentfully or soulfully lodge. Where verbal recurrences are distressed, they are carried as scabs, encrustations, calcification, cuts. If inner speech can sing, it can also tirelessly whisper, mutter, contemplate under its breath to itself, and obsessively reproach itself. It can angrily fondle those names it had once been called. If there's a habitual (if not inevitable) closeness between accusation and interpellation, there's also an echolalic, echoic aspect to interpellation itself. Persecutory interpellation's shadow falls well beyond the instant of its articulation. There are ghosts of the word which always haunt any present moment of enunciation, rendering that present already murmurous and thickly populated. Perhaps "the psyche" is recalled voices as spirit voices manifesting themselves clothed in the flesh of words, and hallucinated accusation may underscore some factually heard accusation. There is in effect a verbal form of post-traumatic stress disorder, marked by unstoppable aural flashbacks. Here anamnesia, unforgetting, is a linguistic curse of a disability. We hear much about the therapeutics of retrieved memory. The inability to *forget*, too, has been classified as a neurological illness.[5]

If language spills to flood everywhere, if it has no describable "beyond," such a broadly true claim can't tell us exactly how it operates on its near side and why its apparent innerness is so ferocious. The reach of a malevolent word's reverberation is incalculable; it may buzz in the head of its hearer in a way that far exceeds any impact that its utterer had in mind. Yet its impress may be weak. Or it may feed melodramas of an apparent addiction to domestic-as-linguistic violence: imagine someone who habitually ends up in a position of pleading with those deaf to all her appeals to act humanely, when it was long clear that they would not do so, yet at those dark moments it seemed to her that her whole possibility of existence was at stake in extracting a humane word from them, although in the past this had always proved impossible. She compulsively redesigns a scenario in which her question "Am I a bad person?" can be asked and answered in its own unhappy terms; for she cannot get her ancient interrogation taken seriously by someone who's not already her opponent; anyone else would rephrase her question, returning it to her to demonstrate its hopelessness. Only she can undo it. Meanwhile if she persists in posing it as it stands, it will only receive an affirmative answer. Then must the force of "the psychic" be isolated here, if the unrelenting person to whom she presents her hopeless appeal is always rediscovered with a terrible reliability, if some damaging interlocutor conveniently appears and reappears for her—while she, the impassioned questioner, labors as if to discover grounds for believing, despite her own sound memories of actual events, that such cruelty could not really have happened?

To continue in this (fatally exhilarating) vein of psychologizing speculation—the capacity of lacerating accusation to indwell may be such that while its target is fearful that it may be true, she's also fearful that it may *not* be true, which would force the abandonment of her whole story. As if in order to "justify" the decades of unhappiness that it has caused her, she almost needs the accusation to be correct—as much as in the same breath, she vehemently repudiates it. Perhaps she would rather take the blame on herself for the harm of the past, because it has already and irretrievably been visited upon her, than to admit it had happened arbitrarily, in that she was then (as a child) truly helpless, an accidental object lying in the path of the assault. Perhaps the need for the accusation to be true, as well as to be simultaneously fought against, is in part her wish to have some rationale, and hence less of frightening contingency as the only explanation for the damage. Perhaps her pleadings for exoneration are also pleadings to have some logic underlying the blame laid bare, so that at last she can grasp and understand it. Hence her tendency to ask repeatedly, "But then why am I, as you tell me I am, an evil person?" There is an anxiety of interpellation, in which its subject ponders incessantly to herself "Am I that name; am I really one of those?" Her query, while it interrogates the harsh attribution, stays under its rigid impress. She needs to find those to whom she can address it and have it taken seriously, despite its capacity to provoke their irritation; this is why recalcitrantly obdurate people will always prove her "best" (that is, least malleable) addressees. She is reluctant to be emancipated from her distressing situation, only because that rescue would makes retrospective nonsense out of a wrong that she was forced to live out as if it had a rationale. Her attachment to the apparent truth inherent in her damnation (even while she nervously denies it) is that in order to make sense of the misery it has caused, she must know it to have been deserved. To have that mimesis of logic taken away from her in retrospect, to be shorn of its "necessity" in the name of her own emancipation is hard—despite the fact that she also profoundly disbelieved in it. For a long time she has struggled intently to convey intelligibility to the damage in the moment that she underwent it, as if there had to be a truth in it. This is a difficult point, and I'm not hinting at any masochistic notion of hers that her pain is deserved, is her own fault—but am simply describing her wish for there to have been some necessity to it, in order to justify it in retrospect.

These last two paragraphs have mimicked a train of speculation as to why, for some purely imaginary heroine of pathos, another's bitter words might have come to be entertained gravely by her. Yet if we're inquiring what exists already that chimes within its target in order for lacerating interpellation to work, the pathology of that accusation itself might accompany our habitual attention to the weaknesses of the accused. An air of reason makes its fatal appearance whenever accusation insistently claims that it is speaking a purely rational cause and effect in its sentence "You are this bad thing, because I say so." The fantasy of formulaic interpellation is that it's only addressing the target which stands before it, whereas its own temporality is badly askew.[6] Then the distorting work of repeated echo may happen for the hearer too: "I've heard this accusation before, so it must hold some truth." Compelled to seek out any logic in the charges against her, she may desperately try to impose some sequence upon what is badly skewed. Perhaps her will to unearth some reason within cruelty will mean that she won't ever detect and register anything intelligible in whatever benign utterances might later come her way. But now we have slipped straight back onto the terrain of speculative psychology again. Next we might try turning it, not onto the target, but onto the utterer of the bad word.

Accusers Themselves Are Forcibly Spoken

It is the cruel gift of the malignant word to linger and echo as if fully detached from its original occasion, whose authoritative hostility I might by now, having recognized it as such, have dethroned. For the word itself still retains its reverberating autonomy, despite my potential overthrow of its speaker. This fact may offer one answer to the suspicion that accusation can retain me in its clutches only because I am especially emotionally pliable in the face of the authority of the Other. The word, instead, may be the real Other. The Other may be cut down to size as words, and dedramatized to lowercase.

A difficulty with theories of the capitalized Other is that they short-circuit the complexity of influences, suggesting a narrowed dialectic, since they function as descriptions of a fantasied mastery which operates within and on the singular figure of the self. But my "I" also always emerges from somewhere else, before the congealing of the Other, and across some history of linguistic exchanges prior to my mastery of words.[7] I am the residue of echoes which precede my cohering and imbue my present being with a shadowiness. These aural shadows may be dispelled, but they may thicken and assume deeper powers of obscurantism. This uncertainty also troubles my accuser equally—perhaps worse. Which is not to deny that there is domination; but we could remember that the big Other of theorized fantasy is also mapped onto the mundane lowercase other in the daily world, those ordinary human others who are also produced by the script of rage, driven along by its theatrical autopilot. The accuser, too, is spoken.

Wittgenstein, a nervously driven questioner himself, brooded over the psychology of compulsive philosophical doubt: "Why should anyone want to ask this question?"[8] The same musing could be turned toward the accuser as a phenomenon: "Why ever should anyone want to speak with this violence?" But there's another thought which sidelines such an interrogation of my accuser's motives: the reflection that he is dispossessed of his own words in advance. The rhetoric of rage speaks him mechanically and remorselessly. However much the accuser feels himself to triumph in the moment of his pronouncement, he is prey to echo. For, as Wallace Stevens neatly observed of the cavernous grandeur of inner oratory, "When the mind is like a hall in which thought is like a voice speaking, the voice is always that of someone else."[9] The orator of violence is merely an instrument of dictation by tics and reflexes. There's nothing gratifyingly original about the language of attack, in which old speech plays through the accuser; it's the one who speaks the damage who becomes its sounding board. (I'm not inching toward a sneaking sympathy for the utterer of hate: that he himself is not remotely in possession of his language does nothing whatsoever to soften his words as they streak through him to crash onto their target.) Rage speaks monotonously. The righteousness of wrathful diction's vocabulary sorely restricts it, the tirade marked by that lack of reflection which alone lets the raging speaker run on and on. Once any awareness of his repetitiousness creeps over him, rather than feel vindicated by the tradition which is driving him, he's more likely to feel embarrassed enough to stop. His fury may be exaggerated by his helplessness at being mastered by his own language (whether or not he gives this description to his subjugation). For the language of anger is so dictatorial that it won't allow him to enjoy any conviction that he's voicing his own authenticity. Meanwhile, my very existence as the butt of his accusation is maddening to him, since under his onslaught, I'm apparently nothing for myself any longer but am turned into a mere thing-bearer of his passion. This is almost irrespective of my own passivity or my retaliation; it's because his utterance has, in its tenor, thrown me down. For the rage speaker, I can have no life left in me, or rather none of that combative life that he needs to secure his own continuing linguistic existence for himself. Attacked, I'm rendered discursively limp, but no real relief can be afforded to my adversary by what he has produced as my rag doll quiescence. The more intense the anger, the less the sense of any agency its utterer possesses, until eventually he feels himself to be the "true victim" in the affair. Hence that common combination of rage with self-pity: a lachrymose wrath. In the light of all this, the injunction to "get in touch with your anger" is hardly the therapeutically liberating practice its proposers assume. Instead, the following variant on the Parisian language school's exhortation, cited earlier, that we should master language before it masters us—"master the language of anger before it masters you"—would prove more emancipating.

But what about being the bad speaker myself? There's an experience that could be described as a linguistic occasion, of being poised somewhere halfway between "language speaks me" and "I speak language." It is the flashing across the mind of words which fly into the head as if they somehow must be said. A clump of phrases shape their own occasion, which swells toward articulation. But I can stop their translation into speech; when maxims are actually uttered aloud, then something else has already given these wordy impulses a currency and licensed their entry into a world of ordered fantasy. This "something else" runs close to the question of somewhere else. Where is the place where language works? A doubtful contrast of inner and outer haunts the puzzle of whether I speak (from the inside outward) or whether I am spoken (from the outside in). This old tension between speaking language and being spoken by it still stretches uncertainly; neither the topography of language's extrusion from the speaker's mouth like ectoplasm, nor its companion, the topography of linguistic entry from the outside, seems an apt resolution. The latter offers a vision of penetration through the ear, like that persuasive Byzantine myth of the annunciation and conception, in which a falling star has shot the ear of the patient Virgin Mary. Sometimes, in an attempt to resolve such puzzles of the place of speech, its polarities get folded together so that the conventionally outer traverses the conventionally inner. Here, for instance: "This passion of the signifier now becomes a new dimension of the human condition in that it is not only man who speaks, but that in man and through man it speaks, that his nature is woven by effects in which is to be found the structure of language, of which he becomes the material, and that therefore there resounds in him, beyond what could be conceived of by a psychology of ideas, the relation of speech."[10] How does such a resonance work in respect of bad words? If words themselves can neatly exemplify the concept of extimacy, in that they are good candidates to be that trace of externality, the foreign body lodged at the very heart of psychic life, nevertheless our impression of an unalloyed inwardness in the case of inner speech is still acute. Despite the attractions of conceiving language as lying out there and lunging in from the outside to speak the speaker, we still sense that we fish up our inner words, or dredge them up. But in the case of recalled damaging speech, it's less like a trawling expedition to plumb some depth, but more of its rising up unbidden, kraken-like, to overwhelm and speak us. Yet at the same time we can also understand this unconscious to come from the outside, in the shape of the common and thoroughly external unconscious of unglamorous language. This mutates into what we experience as our profoundly inner speech. Or as Volosinov (who by the word *ideological* appears to mean the whole world of signs and gestures)[11] tautly formulated it: "Psychic experience is something inner that becomes outer, and the ideological sign, something outer that becomes inner. The psyche enjoys extraterritorial status in the organism. It is a social entity that penetrates inside the organism of the individual person."[12] These shards of imported sociality as bad words remain as impersonal traces in me, in the way that swearing is impersonal; I have not thought them up, they are derivations, clichéd fragments of unoriginality which have lodged in my skull. Usually my verbal memory isn't bland or kindly, or even discreet in its recall. Linguistic shrapnel can lie embedded for years, yet still, as old British soldiers from the First World War reportedly used to say, "give me gyp in damp weather." Still, language is not exactly speaking me at these points—for, unlike the swear word that escapes me when I hammer my thumb, I retain some capacity to not utter it. A single speech event doesn't work in isolation, but darts into the waiting thickness of my inner speech to settle into its dense receptivity. It may become a furious dialogue where I'll plead with some imagined inward other; its script grows heavy with his antagonism, which it preserves in me. My subsequent distress is rehearsed intently and silently under my breath, in a darker version of Volosinov's more benevolent persuasion: "Therefore the semiotic material of the psyche is preeminently the word—inner speech. Inner speech, it is true, is intertwined with a mass of other motor reactions having semiotic value. But all the same, it is the word that constitutes the foundation, the skeleton of inner life. Were it to be deprived of the word, the psyche would shrink to an extreme degree: deprived of all other expressive activities, it would die out altogether."[13]

My swollen (because word-stuffed) psyche can, however, assume the most unbecoming shapes. Some graceless prose of the world has got me in it grip, and my word-susceptible faculty is seized and filled up by it. It's a neurolinguistic circus, this wild leaping to my tongue of banally correct responses, bad puns, retold jokes to bore my children, and undiscerning quotes. To this list could be added many other kinds of stock formulas, in the shape of racist utterance, idle sexism, and other readymades. Inner language is not composed of graceful musing, but of disgracefully indiscriminate repetition, running on automatic pilot. Nevertheless, even if such reflections mean that I'm displaced as an original thinker, I'm not quite evacuated. Even if my tawdry inner language is thinking me (although *thought* is too dignified a term for such gurglings), there's many a slip between inner thought and lip. It's certainly speaking *in* me; but I can subdue it before it fully speaks *me*, I can edit or inhibit the invading words. I am an enforced linguistic collaborator, but only insofar as a long parade of verbal possibilities marches across my horizons. Thought is made in the mouth, but it can also be halted before it passes the lips. And if it isn't, this is hardly an expression of my spontaneity, but rather of my consent to language's orders. Uttering bad words entails an especial passivity of allowing myself to be spoken by automated verbiage, by an "it is speaking in me." If I don't moderate my bad words, my supposedly authentic expression of my feeling consists merely in my obedience to the rising of what is ready made to the tongue. I'm not literally compelled to speak my love, my despair, or my cynicism. Uttered aggression happens when something in me has licensed the articulation of my linguistic impulses into more than flickers. An expression flashes over me and it will have its way, but only if I don't throw it out. That's the extent of the action of my linguistic will; it is no powerful author of its own speech. It comes puffing up in the wake of the inner linguistic event to deal with its violence, to assent to it or demur, or to ascribe some given sentiment or abrogate to myself that standard echoing opinion. What it takes for me, apropos being or not being a bad speaker myself, is not to be a beautiful soul with the hem of my skirts drawn aside from the mud of linguistic harm, but to elect whether to broadcast or to repress the inward yet still thoroughly worldly chattering of imported speech that fills me.

The Word as Thing

Gripped by visions of exuberance swelling into parsimony, Hegel wrote: "Speech and work are outer expressions in which the individual no longer keeps and possesses himself within himself, but lets the inner get completely outside of him, leaving it at the mercy of something other than himself. For that reason we can say with equal truth that these expressions express the inner too much, as that they do so too little . . ."[14] Such a reflection seems to lean toward an antiexpressivist stance, in which a notion of language's natural "expressivity" becomes terribly misleading, either because my utterance is too immediately saturated with me, or is too radically separated from me and is under the sway of whatever carries my words away and out of the range of my intentions. It would be bad naming in particular, through its overblown immediacy, which "does not therefore provide the expression which is sought"[15] and lacks that finally productive self-alienation which pertains (at least in the spasmodically softer focus of the "Hegelian" view) to language proper. In this, Language or Word is Spirit. And if in addition we hold the word to be also historical and material, then the cruel word must also call us into social being, if of a deathly kind. As for the possibility of our resisting it, the language hangs there, supremely indifferent as to whether it is resisted or not. What's more critical for what we could roughly call the Hegelian word view is that to ignore language's sociality would go violently against the way of language in the world. Sociality, of course, is not sociability. On the aspect of making people up, one post-Hegelian has claimed,

> What I seek in speech is the response of the other. What constitutes me as subject is my question. In order to be recognised by the other, I utter what was only in view of what will be. In order to find him, I call him by a name that he must assume or refuse in order to reply to me. . . . But if I call the person to whom I am speaking by whatever name I choose to give him, I intimate to him the subjective function that he will take on again in order to reply to me, even if it is to repudiate this function.[16]

In this manner, Lacan continues to emphasize, I install him as a subject.

Yet we might demur here, in respect of malediction. For hatred aims not at any animated exchange with a respondent, but at that person's annihilation. My defense against serious verbal onslaught, then, could well adopt an analogous tactic of impersonality, and espouse a principled nonengagement with the proffered scenario of (hostile) recognition. I'll ignore the utterer, the better to dissect the utterance. To isolate the word as thing, to inspect it and refuse it, demands a confident capacity to act unnaturally toward language, which normally functions as an energetic means of exchange. Bad words' peculiarly seductive distraction incites me to slip toward self-scrutiny, because another's angry interpellation so readily slides into becoming my own self-interpellation, where a thousand inducements to self-description, self-subjectification, and self-diagnosis are anyway waiting eagerly at its service.[17] But if I simply act "naturally" toward these lures of the bad word, by treating it as any token of exchange and recognition between speakers, I'll be thrown down by it. Then how may I shield myself from its furious resonances? If I don't want to stay petrified by it, then instead I have to petrify it— and in the literal sense. That is, I'll assert its stony character.

Verbal aggression may seem, at first, to be only formally language, and scarcely that at all. It resembles a stone hurled without reflection, which the furious thrower has snatched up just because it lay to hand. The target can't deflect the blow, but will be spared its aftereffects because she realizes the impersonal quality of the thing. The word considered as stone will shock but not break her. The denunciation hurts on impact but later it weakens, as its target sees there is only an accidental link between what was hurled and the will to hurl. She realizes that the bad word is not properly "expressive" of the speaker's impulse to aggressive speech (it cannot be, since "there is always at once too much as too little"[18]) while the impulse needs to be understood in itself and independently of its instrument. So if I decide to embrace this defensive strategy, I can inform the malignant word that it's not really a word by the strenuous artifice of detaching it from the person who pronounced it (dispatching him, for the time being, to wander stripped of his tongue in the idiosyncratic shades of his own psychology). This is my opening gambit. Next I'll turn to contemplate the malevolent word, now separated from its speaker, and quivering furiously like an abandoned dart lost to the guiding authority of the hand that threw it. Now I have to aim at its death, in the same way that, as a spoken accusation, it had aimed at my death. I can kill it only by artificially abstracting it from the realm of language altogether (although I realize perfectly well that human utterance always bristles with such weapons). I have to let it go indifferently, as a thing to which I myself have become as indifferent as the bad word itself had really been, all along, to me. The *accuser* was not indifferent, then. But the afterlife of malignant speech is vigorously spectral, quite independent of its emission at the instant of rage. The bad word flaps in its vampire's afterlife in the breast of its target, who can try to quell it, but "cannot go the length of being altogether done with it to the point of annihilation: in other words, he only *works* on it."[19] The spoken savagery hovers there still. However can its target "work" on it? Stripping the speaker away from the word brings it into a loneliness, into its prominent isolation from the occasion of its utterance. This act of detaching it returns it to its impersonal communality, and into the dictionary of latent harm, while wrenching it away from its respectably bland and democratic-sounding claim to share in language's supposed intersubjectivity. And as suggested, I can also turn the phenomenology of cruel speaking against my accuser to characterize him as not having been the master, let alone the origin, of his own sadism, but of having been played like a pipe, swayed like a hapless reed. The words that rushed to his tongue were always an ersatz rhetoric. The diction of hatred long precedes its speakers. Meanwhile, I can also recognize his distance from me, his indifference—an indifference which, by now, is not only a spent feeling only coolly attentive to me, but of a psychology which has long since returned to itself, and now wanders about the world intent on its fresh preoccupations, far out of the range of my unhappy surveillance.

But may not my commentary have dealt in too cavalier or too sunnily optimistic a fashion with the hurtful word's curious duration? I've been implying that the intention to hurt can be treated by its target as almost irrelevant, and that there's an impersonality in hate speech which can be harnessed for protective and quasi-therapeutic purposes. But the injured person may well feel that the aggressive speech was heavy with a plan to hurt her and was calculatedly aimed at the gaps in her armor; how, then, could her conviction of this deliberate intent to cause pain be at all eased by the thesis that bad words also enthrall, in all senses, their own speaker? To which reasonable objection I'd reply that my speculations are indeed an exercise in mounting a defense, and they do sideline this question of recognizing a pointed intention to destroy. But they also usefully detach the fact of an intent to hurt from any assumption that the angry speaker controls the repercussions of his words; for the targeted person might well assume his invincibility and so run the risk of crediting the violent speaker with more than he really possesses. What's more, following the Stoic principle of discerning what's up to you, or what lies within your proper sphere of concern, you'd do far better to return the other to the vagaries of his own passion, rather than pursue him or her in your imagination with interrogations about motives: "Leave another's wrongdoing where it lies."[20]

Yet there's still a further turn in the work that has to be done. Love's work pales in comparison with Hate's work, in the sense of the legacy of being hated, which condemns its recipients to an iniquitous toil of elucidation.[21] Having returned the bad word to its waiting niche in the stout dictionary of unkindness, I'll need not only to return the speaker to the accident of himself, but I have to attempt a further labor of emancipation for myself. I must recognize his indifference to my present tormented memories of his old utterances, and return him to an absolute indifference in which I abandon him, even in my speculations. I, too, need to "have done with the thing altogether."[22] But to succeed in having done with it demands a prior and ferocious dwelling on it, which first unsparingly remembers the reverberating word as word—yet only in order to restore its truly impersonal quality, to return it to the generality of utterance from whence it came, and to acknowledge its superb and sublimely indifferent capacity to take me or leave me. That is, I'll get rid of understanding myself as "the suffering person." And I shall manage to give up that unhappy and unproductive self-designation only at the same stroke in which I can fully grasp the impersonality of the bad word. This I'll come to do as a consequence of registering its cruelty, letting it sink completely into me—that is, by going straight through the route of the profoundly personal. Only then, through entering its peculiar blackness unprotected, can I sever the word from its speaker in order to imaginatively return him to his true contingency and to his present cheerily amnesiac indifference to my continuing lacerations by his verbal attack, the occasion of which has doubtless long since escaped his mind.

By this stage, I've gradually and waveringly relinquished what's standardly taken to be a Hegelian concept of language, because it would have been too optimistic, since too tranquilly intersubjective, for the task at hand. Now instead, some of Hegel's own and less sunny descriptions of language as a "stain," a "contagion," and the ground of "a universal infection" of selves may receive their testing ground on the territory of damaging words.[23] (Admittedly, there are pleasant kinds of stains, and perhaps even happy contagions; but Hegel's scattered metaphor of infection is harder to recuperate.) Let's follow its logic. To enable my release, my initial infection by the bad word with virulent fear and the most relentless self-doubt is necessary. A mild anxiety won't suffice. My entire self-conception must have tottered. "If it has not experienced absolute fear, but only some lesser dread, the negative being has remained for it something external, its substance has not been infected by it through and through."[24] With this apparently paradoxical association of language with infection, we're dealing, in short, with the true sociability of language—as contagion, as a mouth disease. To recover, as I must, from accusation's damaging impact on me, I can't effectively stand lonely proof against it, but instead have to admit something that so far I have been reluctant to consider: that, *exactly as my injury*, it enjoys a fully languagelike status. Now, in this moment, I have abandoned all my earlier humanist strategy of seeing the bad word as a hurled stone and therefore not as true language. Instead I've begun to understand that the bad word is an indifferently speaking stone. In sum, that harsh language evinces a sheer indifference both to me and also to my accuser, an ultimately sociable impersonality, and a sadism, that (uninterested in me though it is) has worked successfully on me while it also suffers its own corrosion and decay.

But if instead I overlook all these characteristics of language, and meditate solely "psychologically," I'll examine only my own idiosyncratically undefended subjecthood by discovering some prior susceptibility within my depths, an early wound which is the key to my constant vulnerability—as if therein I could unearth some meaning to my haunting by the word and free myself. The trouble with this speculation is that the linguistic structure of my childhood verbal wounding was and is exactly the same as that which vexes me now; when I was two years old, there was no "purely psychic" naming for me even then, but an interpellation which, always linguistic, was thereby always affective. Infancy's learning to speak is also entangled in parental emotions—the hostility, anxiety, lucidity, mildness. But this evident fact only reinforces my persuasion that the linguistic and the psychic are neither separable, nor to be subsumed one under another. If there is now the same scenario, an original injury which I relive, its endless reanimation in me is not surprising, given the paucity of my capacities for self-protection then. That is, there's not a chronology of depth of my early (psychic) injury which precedes, founds, and accounts for some later and categorically different (linguistic) vulnerability—other than that vital history of my childish and necessary dependence on others' affective words.

All of these considerations which might help to deflate lacerating speech—considerations of the vatic nature of the language itself, and the transient emotion of its speaker driven by the rhetoric he deploys—might be equally applied to a recollected "I love you." The erratic love-speaker claims to have meant his declarations *then*, but now he has changed his feelings and disavows everything. And he protects himself from the charge of fickleness by avowing the innocent contingency of his declaration, rather in the way that to protect oneself from the hate speaker, one considers how the bite of his words might be eased through a recognition of their awful contingency. If we compare the aftermath of hearing "I love you" with the aftermath of hearing "I hate you," in both instances the hearer may fight to sever the utterance from its vanished utterer. With the former declaration, the struggle is to find compensation in the teeth of impermanence (those words were definitely said to me, so at least I can be sure that once I was loved even though their speaker has gone). And with the latter, to find protection from the risk of permanence (those words were directed at me, but it wasn't especially me who was hated, I just accidentally got in that speaker's way).

The stoic's route to consolation, however, can't follow this path of detecting necessity in the instance of her being loved, but contingency in the case of her being hated. She is more prone to regard both love speech and hate speech alike as workings of that language which (to return to our Parisian language school's slogan) we've not the faintest hope of mastering before it masters us. Nonetheless, we can still elect to suffer our subjugation moodily and darkly, or we can treat it more lightly and indifferently, as a by-product of the disinterested machinations of language. To espouse such a notion of linguistic impartiality in this way is, I think, the sounder course. I could be more effectively freed from damaging words by first confronting and then conceding my own sheer contingency as a linguistic subject. I am a walker in language. It's only through my meanders and slow detours, perhaps across many decades, toward recognizing language's powerful impersonality—which is always operating despite and within its air of a communicative "intersubjectivity"—that I can "become myself." Yet I become myself only by way of fully accepting my own impersonality, too—as someone who is herself accidentally spoken, not only by violent language, but by any language whatsoever—and who, by means of her own relieved recognition of this very contingency, is in significant part released from the powers of the secretive and unspeakable workings of linguistic harm.

———

TWO

"What I Want Back Is What I Was": Consolation's Retrospect

———

*

"If a horse in its elation should say 'I am beautiful' it would be bearable."[1] Epictetus, the Stoic philosopher, doesn't go on to say that if a human were to utter the same sentiment, it would be unbearable: only that the horse's owner shouldn't try to take credit himself for the gratuitous beauty of his animal, or try to bask in those equine good looks which, owned by him, aren't his. The horse, though, in its jubilation can get away with boasting.

There's a noticeable awkwardness about the mention of human physical beauty; its embarrassment can include a fear of lapsing into the vanity deplored alike by the Old Testament and by some feminisms, for feminism has had its own good reasons for reticence, if not for a slide into severity. This common hesitation in naming beauty isn't simply the wish to steer clear of laying arrogant claims to distinction; for someone can say, not boastfully but in the spirit of mentioning a contingent fact, "I used to be a strong swimmer." But there does seem to be something especially stubborn, unmentionable, about beauty's indwelling independence. The fact that, once it has become a lost thing, it becomes clear that it was never owned isn't enough to characterize faded beauty's peculiarities. For the same holds true, for instance, of youth. It's extremely difficult to feel yourself to be young at the actual time you are. Certainly I was never a child.

These pages will skip all but one small aspect of this matter of who or what can claim beauty. Their aim, disappointingly, won't be to proffer beauty tips, but rather to brood over the linguistic incitement to retrospective identification through the imagined retrieval of what one once was (a business which, in its evocation of a moment which never existed, rather inverts a fantastic logic of self-exculpation: "If only we had known at the time that there were no weapons there!"). I'll look only at an extremely common sentence of regret for lost physical beauty: at that strange bending of time involved in saying inwardly "Yes, I suppose in the past I must have been beautiful, as people used to say, although at the time I never saw it." To meditate on this ordinary thought is by no means to despise it. Slipping into the retrospective-fantastic mood may be positively benign, for instance, a compensating refusal to treat any-one now as harshly as I was myself treated then. (And there can be far riskier contents than mere vanity to some declared "realization," such as convictions of revelation: "Now I see that all along I was a favored son of God, though formerly I was blind to this shining truth.") But, leaving aside such conversions, in general it would be foolish to tut over retro-spective self-shaping. This is how the language of self-characterization often operates: backwards.[2] It would be vacuous, too, to condemn our attempts at a little distraction from the approach of death with sentences such as "After all, I suppose I must have been something of a beauty when I was young," or at least, where you know no such a claim can be staked, the lament "Compared to what I am now, they should have seen me then!" — which is always true. For timor mortis is ever at hand, and this fear of death will only intensify: as in Shakespeare's

> The wrinkles which thy glass will truly show
> Of mouthèd graves will give thee memory[3]

Still, there's something of a taboo or an unnameability about the gradual erosion of whatever we tentatively feel we once had by way of beauty, a silence which, unsurprisingly, persists irrespective of the enor-mous new industries of repair and regeneration. This anxiety over the eclipse of your looks is exhaustively catered to (and, in the process, mag-nified) yet is itself a dread scarcely mentioned. A culture so tolerant and encouraging of public vanity remains strikingly silent on the question of the fear underlying it. Instead, how beauty's ordinary loss is silently spoken is the point at which the consolations of illusion meet and for-tify the illusions of consolation. If their encounter produces a blankness liable to sink into depressive shame, arguably this adds to an unvoiced vertigo of the everyday; what more, though, could our thinking aloud about it do?

The Sentence of Retrospect

For the purposes of illustrating this grammar of retrospect, let's imagine a puppet (for the purposes of argument here, a caricature will have to do) which is oddly equipped with inner speech: this someone longs to get back something from his former days, although he knows that then he was never confident of it, it eluded him, people seemed to be drawn to something in him but he never knew what it was, never had any means of grasping it himself, but it must have been something which now, in his late middle age, might be returned to him by means of his renewed recall in which he might at last seize and savor it. All this longing murmurs energetically in him, despite the fact that his is a memory which has nothing remembered behind it. His invention-cum-discovery of his former fineness runs close to being autobiography as thanatology (for telling one's life story through what college courses tend to call Life Writing is, given its trajectory, Death Writing). His "then I must have been that beautiful thing" is a half-knowing indulgence in something forbidden to him to utter in the present tense, yet allowed by virtue of its apparently innocuous assignment to his past. It also fashions how, in future, he'll come to allow himself to understand himself. If it soaks his present in nostalgia, nevertheless this sentence will, with an odd temporal elasticity, readily become a nostalgia for the future. For his own future, that is; his unspoken "OK, now I'll agree to have been what I used to be told I was" is a highly convoluted kind of self-recognition — it's a concession which also has the shape of a sentence of *confession*. "Yes, I too was once beautiful, although when I was young I could never grasp that": what's happening when he "recalls" this condition that he also knows he could never have lived? He could not, because, irrespective of the reality of his fine looks, and irrespective of whether someone is perceived by others as gorgeous or ill-favored, he is never in possession of his own appearance.

These days, however, a burgeoning beauty industry for men offers to "restore" to him something he never previously enjoyed. His former looks he could not help; then he was admired for something far beyond his ordering (whatever his expenditure on elegant barbers, Armani, and moisturizers). If there was once some traveling of beauty across him, he can claim no more credit for it than could the owner of the horse mentioned by Epictetus for the gloss of that animal. For the man of retrospect, too, in reality an accident was traced over his skin. This accident he will assume and will try to have organized, but belatedly and falsely. "What I want back is what I was"—this strong line of Sylvia Plath's, if wrenched from its context and used instead as a model sentence about our longing to retrieve our lost looks, embodies an untruth; its speaker was *never* a dweller in that past.[4] And here a remembered compliment from thirty years ago springs to the mind of this caricatured man. It had caused him to feel intensely awkward, even humiliated, at the time. Some shame at hearing "you are beautiful" made it shocking. There was embarrassment at being told this. Worse, he heard it as an accusation. His present bashfulness stems partly from his own fiction of having been it, partly from the helplessness of a remembered accidental glaze or a shimmer around him, no thanks to him. What he had glimpsed then, in the alarm of his beauty, was his own exteriorization. Whatever was this thing which they, apparently, perceived in him, but which he could not see in himself? He unearths a partial answer in the perspectival nature of seeing, as Merleau-Ponty has it: "The enigma is that my body simultaneously sees and is seen. . . . It is a self through confusion, narcissism, through inherence of the one who sees in that which he sees, and through inherence of sensing in the sensed—a self, therefore, that is caught up in things, that has a front and a back, past and a future."[5] Our puppet contorts himself until he feels he too glimpses it, the thing they must have seen in him, but he does so at the cost of surrendering himself to an exteriority in which he imagines himself seen as a thing "through their eyes." By this stage he's poised perilously close to becoming the sex object of the old feminist critique. Yet all these beholders of his, demeaning or admiring, are at the same time themselves his projections. Perhaps he's realized himself, rightly, to be the terrain across which beauty had once rushed, and has by now rushed away for good. Or at the least, the dwindling of whatever faint claims he might have had to even bearable looks remains hellish enough to him. But he was always dispossessed of his own beauty. No one has theirs. Not, though, because beauty is "relative." But because even the most conventionally exquisite creature is not the author of its appearance. And this dispossession is prior to and indifferent to the furiously applied arts of the cosmetic surgeon, the rigors of the personal trainer. If our illustrative man eventually adopts as his own what he hopes were once others' impression of his old self, he can't truly do this as if accepting a revelation. He can only make a concession. He concedes to enter an unwinding, where the unlovely present marks of time, the potbellied, the shiny domed, the slack jowled, are reversed to become the approaching phantom of the beautiful youth of what he takes to be others' past perceptions of him. His "recall" of this self is something engineered; no recollection, but more of an agreement to agree — with an evaluation which maybe no one had actually put to him. "Now I'll admit to having been what I was told I was" is a confessional formula verging on bad faith, so well aware is it of handing itself over to the judgments it attributes to others. This falling in with his lost loveliness that he's dreamed reflected in the eyes of others is Thought rejoicing to have had what it intuits it never really had at all. As now he consents to have been that thing, it's in the half-knowledge, at least, that at the time he could not have muttered "I am beautiful" without comical complacency. Perhaps he could have proposed something self-consciously modest (so vitiating any real claim to modesty) such as "at that moment, accidentally, beauty shot across me." But this, if closer to the truth of the thing, is ponderous yet fey. It was only ever bearable for him to be told that he was beautiful if he was loved by the speaker and if, crucially, he loved her (or him) in return. Not exactly because she was blinded to his bodily defects by her passion (although doubtless she was) — but because her passion guaranteed the truth of her utterance as utterance. So he might truly conclude, "Then I was beautiful to that person, but because and only because she cared for me."

Something in him, it seems, has faded now. Younger women's eyes flick past him. Privately, he closely monitors the superior preservation of certain of his friends; for if like Tennyson's woods, the friends decay, the friends decay and fall, some manage to do so with a horrible grace. So he abandons his own recollection of never having had beauty. Instead he hands himself over to what he supposes to have been the perceptions of him by others. Now his effort against his own melancholia brightens up. In a luxury of resignation, he agrees to have been it then.

Dropping this wooden puppet of retrospect, with his neck permanently twisted backward, what next can we do with this syntax he's merely served to model? The odd tense of dimmed beauty could lead us straight into ruinous sentimentalizing, by which we're on the shore of the Venice lido like Dirk Bogarde in the role of Gustav von Aschenbach, withered cheeks awash with tears and mascara as we gaze toward the exquisitely indifferent boy.[6] It could, though, lead us in more astringent directions. First, a short detour round milder routes.

Attempted Consolations: A Rapid Sketch

The sentence of retrospect is propelled by its impulse to console its utterer. The lightest survey reveals many other modes of attempted consolation, plausible or not, for diminished beauty. The quickest means — if only it would reliably work — is through resignation. And resignation chews over such ordinary thoughts as these: Physical beauty is gaily undemocratic in its distribution. Appeals to its "cultural relativism" don't even begin to disturb that brutal truth. If an elongated neck is held to be a supremely beautiful thing, then within that culture there are, remorselessly, still necks and necks. Nor can newer variants on the old saw "Beauty is in the eye of the beholder" cut much ice, such as studies of the viciousness of "lookism," which demonstrate that better-looking employees earn more; or pleas for the special grace of the elderly; or the folly of intolerance of the physically imperfect. All such well-intentioned efforts only afford to gentlemen, in reaction, the chance to become mechanical comedians, as in this conservatively wry note from Hegel: "Among men, for instance, it is the case that at any rate every bridegroom thinks his bride beautiful, and indeed, perhaps, he alone: though not, it may be, every husband his wife; and that subjective taste for such beauty has no fixed rule, one may hold to be the good fortune of both parties."[7] It's an ordinarily harsh fact that the beauty of the flesh is eroded by time. On this we need not dwell. Chief among false consolations here is that beauty is inner. It is not. It is outer. Fran Lebowitz is right: "All God's children are not beautiful. Most of God's children are, in fact, barely presentable. The most common error made in matters of appearance is the belief that one should disdain the superficial and let the true beauty of one's soul shine through. If there are places on your body where this is a possibility, you are not attractive—you are leaking."[8] A few sturdy souls excepted, most men and women lament the decline of their appearance, irrespective of how their looks started out, since aging doesn't enhance a modest endowment, add polish to the lackluster, or mitigate a birthright of frank ugliness. Sadness at lost looks stubbornly remains, however contested it is through appeals to the cultural variability of beauty, to the need to gracefully accept your natural aging, or to free yourself from the imbalanced market-driven consumption of a rapacious world.

Yet it's striking that this common fate of the flesh is these days discussed only journalistically, and most often through the journalism of sexual difference; although aging bruises the amour-propre of both sexes, it has always been taken to weigh more heavily on women. Now, though, the old sexed gap of anxiety and fear is famously narrowing, as evidenced in the eroticism of male cosmetics and surgical implants, in advertisements' polished six-packs of abdominal muscles, or young lads as objects of a newly lecherous female gaze. As this sexual democratization of worry advances, so does the onset of the ravages of time. The decline, which, according to the memento mori from the copywriters of the body beautiful, begins in your twenties, means that however young you are, you should always make purchases to guard your skin against aging. So you might as well start on your self-preservation, as your worry dictates, at puberty—if not even earlier. Nudging the shelves of weekly pornography, swelling ranks of men's health magazines enable their lessons in how to become handsomer to slip under the more respectable guise of instruction in becoming fitter. The praiseworthy pursuit of health offers a fine alibi for the less admissible pursuit of male beauty. And if any onlookers' objections to such self-beautifying are shot through with a trace of the revulsion which convulsed Jonathan Swift as he annotated women's artifices—"Such gaudy tulips raised from dung"[9]—at least such revulsion can cut both ways today. Here is a happily low form of consolation for one sex: apprehension about their fading looks is virulently infecting the other sex, too.

If all such attempts at resigned thought falter, then a more practical form of consoling yourself is promised by doing repair work. The newish French word *relookage*, or having a makeover, is fetching for an English speaker, since "to look your age" is the lapse that relookage aims to cure. The history of vanity abounds in modes of relookage that are earlier than you'd imagine; today's hands-on consolations of facelifts and Botox injections had their precedents very early in the twentieth century. Cosmetic surgery wasn't, as often supposed, an offshoot of the venerable work of plastic surgeons for war-damaged soldiers; for already by 1903, for instance, injected paraffin wax was being used in Vienna for beautification; the results were hell, but the practice went on for decades.[10] "Such well known doctors as Joseph Safian of New York recall patients begging them in the 1920s to deal with the effects of paraffin wax injected into the face. Hundreds of cosmetic surgeons struggled almost hopelessly to removes masses of facial tissue infiltrated by solidified paraffin wax; the whole permeated part had to be taken away. Corrective work on paraffinomas, as they were called, constituted a major part of the early cosmetic surgeon's practice."[11] There are, though, time-honored and safer forms of the preservation of beauty—such as the *paraffinoma* as Shakespearean sonnet. Here memory itself, if only it can be written down memorably enough, becomes the preserving agent:

> His beauty shall in these black lines be seen
> And they shall live, and he in them still green.[12]

If a whiff of beauty in formaldehyde were the best that cosmetic intervention could secure, all would be petrified, dead. An air of animation seems to be essential for repair work to be effective: hence the cynicism heaped on the excessively face-lifted of today, with their features' frozen immobility. But a more animated, indeed a literally animated, consolation can also lie at hand—through an act of vicarious possession in rebirth. Another of Shakespeare's sonnets addresses his beloved:

> Then of thy beauty do I question make
> That thou among the wastes of time must go.[13]

The answer provided in this lyrical solution to the erosion of the lover's face is clear cut: he should have children in the face of Time, should "breed to brave him." Here Consolation makes its conventional declaration that very well, now someone else in whom the young man has a stake can enact his beauty for him. This parental narcissism is a sanctioned pride in the beauty of one's children. Its half-aware thought that "my son and my daughter are reliving it for me, are being it in my place" is an exemplar of interpassivity and substitutionism, let alone of borderline vampirism. My creature is to reanimate my own expired beauty.

Pragmatic resignation to our lost looks may arrive, too, through the thoroughly worldly attempt to avoid making ourselves look very foolish. The young Jonathan Swift's cautionary "When I Come to Be Old" lists those tedious mannerism of age he intends to shun: "Not to boast of my former beauty, or strength, or favor with Ladyes, &c."[14] But nostalgia's weakness will out. If making a confession is often a secretly gratifying activity, to confess to a common fragility in our longing for lost advantage is especially so. Human, all too human! Still, not *too* human; if beauty's only residue is its fifty-something dispossessed owner's unreconstructed mannerisms of boyish seductiveness, the results are most unhappy. In short, a great deal that's absurd in this business of getting back what you never had in the first place could be rewritten as smooth parody. As if in some saccharine and languorously sardonic lyric from Lorenz "Larry" Hart:[15]

> To lay a claim to your past beauty is distasteful
> Yet wiping out all reference to it's rather wasteful
>
> Sometimes I guess my eyes were truly luminous
> In the mirror, and my breasts kind of voluminous
>
> At which point Beauty, supposed to be numinous
> Swayed on the brink of getting frankly glutinous
>
> Yet when he'd muttered to me, You're so beautiful
> I'd just assumed that he was simply being dutiful
>
> So was he then, or I am now, really being truthful
> To find OK what I'd found wrong when youthful?

—and so on, illustrating the old intimacy between beauty and its parody, as in its well-known complicity with drag. Let's look for something more bracing.

Other consolations of philosophies, formal and informal, offer a toughly resigned acceptance of your own lost looks—like the realism which admits that to have what's now fled was, at the time, no picnic. Better, for a woman, her present benign and unenvious beaming into younger women's strollers than what had preceded it. Only when sunk far into the relaxing invisibility of her middle age may she forget her earlier hell of being repeatedly felt up on public transport, mortified by builders' catcalls, pursued by grimly compulsive attentions and unrelenting comment, as if her passing in the street had to incite at least a verbal reaction, as if the form of sexual admiration had always to be aggression.

A brief turn to the Stoics may quiet her ratty recall.

Stoicism and the Limits of Self-Care

That modern romantic note of Keats's "She dwells with Beauty—Beauty that must die" is, as it proclaims, soused in intoxicated melancholy.[16] Such a sensibility would have been tersely refused by the stoical attitude. To be clay was simply the lot of the human animal. As Epictetus declared, "you are a little soul carrying a corpse."[17] For the matter of our death, when the universe wanted our bodies it would take them. Better, then, to prepare to yield them. How to live well, meanwhile, in the teeth of this knowledge?

A sense of proportionate responsibility helped; so to avoid mistaken claims to owning your beauty was critical for graceful living. The Roman writer Boethius, in his *The Consolation of Philosophy*, follows the Stoics in emphasizing the importance of not abrogating to oneself a beauty which is really gratuitous or which depends on, say, elegant clothing. His figure of Philosophy upbraids her disciple: "Why do you embrace as your own the good things which are outside yourself? Fortune will never make yours what Nature has made to belong to other things."[18] Such an awareness of your radical dispossession from your supposed attributes should be coupled with a concentration on the instant; the truly Stoic response to the blows of accident is to dwell rigorously in the here and now. True self-sufficiency also possesses a principled indifference to its fate. It's to this end that Marcus Aurelius advocates nipping self-sorrow in the bud, in favor of paying a scrupulous attention to living in the world at this very second: "Remember that man lives only in the present, in this fleeting instant: all the rest of his life is either past and gone, or not yet revealed."[19] This conviction that we live best as we live bodily—in the now—wipes out nostalgia, hermeneutics, and all compulsive unearthing of genealogies and determining psychologies of the self. As the classical historian Pierre Hadot elaborates, "Stoics and Epicureans had in common an attitude which consisted in liberating oneself not only from worries about the future but also from the burden of the past, in order to concentrate on the present moment; in order either to enjoy it or to act within it. From this point of view, neither the Stoics nor the Epicureans accorded a positive value to the past."[20] All this entailed a disciplined self-scrutiny, but it was no narcissism of excavating a true self. It was a self-transcendence, reached only by way of passing scrupulously through the self. Introspection was no end in itself, rather a means of getting beyond one's person to the universal reachable through that fierce concentration on the particular. So "interiorization is a going beyond oneself; it is universalization."[21]

This Stoical work of living sharply—not by eliminating the physical self, but by stripping it of pride in a beauty which could never be owned—made self-care turn outward to achieve itself. If a too restricted attention to the self were practiced, then this illuminating movement toward the world would be arrested; and the self would be pushed fatally inward, contrary to Seneca's evocation of plunging yourself into the whole of the world.[22] The unmasterable nature of beauty, and its wilfulness, was underlined by Marcus Aurelius: "Anything in any way beautiful derives its beauty from itself, and asks nothing beyond itself. Praise is no part of it, for nothing is made worse or better by praise."[23] So a neophyte's anxiety at the vulnerability of his own glamour should be redrafted as acceptance of time's indifference to his charms, and to living decorously in the realization of the sheer impersonality of his beauty. True self-care, then, had to be sternly functional. The reason, says Epictetus, for avoiding physical self-neglect is that its consequences would vex others' sensibilities: "What, then is anyone asking you to prettify yourself? By no means, except in those things where our nature requires it; in reason, judgments, actions; but as regards our body, only as far as cleanliness demands, and the avoidance of offence."[24] One Stoical imperative: don't smell. On this point, Epictetus again:

> If nature had trusted a horse to your care, would you have overlooked and neglected him? Now, consider that your body has been committed to you like a horse; wash it, rub it down, make it such that nobody will turn away from it or seek to avoid it. But who does not avoid a man who is dirty, and smells and looks unwholesome, even more than a man who is befouled with dung? The stench of the latter is external and adventitious, but that which arises from want of care comes from within, as though from a kind of inward putrefaction.[25]

A cared-for appearance at least indicated its owner had a grasp of the seemly; so a youth bent on learning philosophy, "with his hair finely dressed,"[26] could be redirected from his preoccupation with his transient looks to the reliable beauty of reason itself. A patently self-neglecting lad, though, afforded enlightenment scant hope: "But if he should come to me befouled, dirty, with whiskers down to his knees, what can I say to him, what sort of comparison can I use to draw him on? . . . For does he in fact aspire to beauty? Does he show any sign of it? Go and argue with a pig, that he should not roll in the mud."[27]

Following these Stoics, then, our duty of modern self-care hardly extends as far as liposuction. But what about the rowing machine? How do we distinguish a virtuous focus on the body from mere relookage; where does a praiseworthy pursuit of fitness shade into the new history of vanity, including the imperative to revamp the pecs and the abs—muscles which, tightened in the gym, are duly mirrored in their contracted names? As "Larry" Hart himself might have put it,

> While I work on getting myself tautly muscular
> My motives aren't so innocently cardiovascular.

One well-known modern reanimation of the idea of self-care appears in Michel Foucault's work as the "practices of the self."[28] But here the specter of the old Stoical minimal ideal suffering gentrification into a charmed self-regard worries Pierre Hadot. For the new version might fall short of that necessary interiorization "inseparably linked to another movement whereby one rises to a higher psychic level, at which one encounters another kind of exteriorisation, another relationship with the 'exterior.' "[29] Instead, claims Hadot, "by focusing his interpretation too exclusively on the culture of the self, the care of the self, and conversion toward the self—more generally by defining his ethical model as an aesthetics of existence—M. Foucault is propounding a culture of the self which is too aesthetic. In other words, this may be a new form of Dandyism, late twentieth-century style."[30] The risk is of a self polished in its exquisite apartness, whereas Stoical self-making had needed no elegant isolation but could well be pursued by means of a public life. Yet we can see that Foucault knows this very well; he writes, "round the care of the self, there developed an entire activity of speaking and writing in which the work of oneself on oneself and communication with others were linked together. Here we touch on one of the most important aspects of this activity devoted to oneself; it constituted, not an exercise in solitude, but a true social practice."[31] Ultimately there is, for both these twentieth-century commentators, a sociable Stoicism which is far from an austere refusal of the world in the name of autonomy.

How would such a Stoicism, opposed to both triumphalism and mourning, respond to our modern aging man's dilemma (to return to the caricatured figure I began with)? It might keep the ancient insistence on Fortune's arbitrariness, by proposing something like this: His beauty, in all its person-marking impersonality, flits across him and is coolly indifferent to him. In the face of its superb disinterest, any vaunted modesty on his part would be a foolish pose to strike. He need not bother to reiterate that his beauty really had nothing to do with him, since, transparently, it hadn't. His sheer contingency in the face of any past aesthetic worth is reconfirmed. He has never, ever, been at the slightest risk of "being beautiful." He is an accident which beauty had stamped as such by passing across him. So he is liberated to enjoy it at a discreet distance, since it has had no need whatsoever of him. A shame, then, if instead of finding his contentment by calmly accepting the accidental, he should mistakenly try to lay retrospective claim to his mislaid possession, his lost beauty—an effort which would yield only the sickly scent of violet cachous. Instead, his true care of the self should take the form of a cheerful indifference to himself. If he could live without depressive hindsight and fully in the moment, he'd be freed from the burden of disinterring and deciphering his past. Instead he could grasp, acutely, where he now lives.

Still, it could be objected that this Stoical will to living purely now is weakened by the problem of just what constitutes a present moment. How long is it? How wide might the concentrated focus of an instant be? A moment of dwelling in the present may also incorporate a long penumbra of dwelling on loss. A vivid part of an instant is its drawing into itself the reverberating past as the impacted persistence of earlier ravages. Or, if faintly, earlier happiness. Since the Stoic has to act in the present, and if we expand the scope of the present to include its echoes of past pain, how do we stem the threatening flood-tide of melancholia? How can Stoicism's recognition of contingency, its recommended graceful and unfussy submission to necessity, and its focus on living in the now, be aligned with melancholia's gravitational pull inside our common sentence of retrospect ("what I want back is what I was") so as to usefully weaken it?

Perhaps there's a prospect in view in which these astringent consolations of Stoicism may be led into reconciliation with our strange if daily syntax of mourning the never-had as a once-having-had.

Consolation and the Syntax of Fantastic Identification

His former beauty is what our aging man has come to grasp as something faded that he will henceforth assume. This resembles a sentence of Lacan's, resplendent in its baroque future anterior tenses: "What is realized in my history is not the past definitive of what was, since it is no more, or even the present perfect of what has been in what I am, but the future anterior of what I shall have been for what I am in the process of becoming."[32] But in our case of extinguished beauty, we've seen that a prominent element of submission to an (actual or imagined) characterization of oneself by others springs up at the very heart of this "what I shall have been." Hence its sanctimonious yet at the same time tremulous tone. A vicariously reached self-interpellation has run through a loop of a recalled or dreamed-up interpellation by others. Absurdity is no bar to such autoventriloquy.[33] And just here, in the appeal to my putative judgment by the rest, in the contorted syntax which, envisaging itself seen by others, turns to whatever it figures as the world's witness, lies the opening for that ambiguously redeeming "social" element espoused by some recent writers on identification.[34]

But it would be an inflated claim that in the case of lost looks we're really dealing with a version of psychoanalytic retrospection, or belatedness: *nachträglichkeit*. We aren't, since there's no misery of an original trauma, reactivated. With the demise of his handsomeness, our subject isn't reencountering an early and suppressed blow which had become inaccessible to him (or if he is said to be, it's too vague a generalization). Freud, considering the phenomenon of nachträglichkeit as what he calls "deferred action," retells a lip-licking tale: "Love and hunger, I reflected, meet at a woman's breast. A young man who was a great admirer of feminine beauty was talking once—so the story went—of the good-looking wet-nurse who had suckled him when he was a baby: 'I'm sorry,' he remarked, 'that I didn't make a better use of my opportunity.' I was in the habit of quoting this anecdote to explain the factor of deferred action in the mechanism of the psychoneuroses."[35] Committed to his own belief in the original sociality of the unconscious, Jean Laplanche (who translates *nachträglichkeit* as "afterwardsness" rather than as "deferred action") elaborates on this story:

> Now the only possible synthesis is to take into account what he [Freud] doesn't take into account, that is, *the wet nurse*. If you don't take into account the wet nurse herself, and what she contributes when she gives the breast to the child—if you don't have in mind the external person, that is, the stranger, and the strangeness of the other—you cannot grasp both directions implicit in afterwardsness. . . . If you try to understand afterwardsness only from the point of view of this man, being first a baby and then an adult, you cannot understand afterwardsness. That is, if you don't start from the other, and from the category of the message, you cannot understand afterwardsness. You are left with a dilemma that is impossible to resolve: either the past determines the future, or the future reinterprets the past.[36]

In the spirit of Laplanche's complication of Freud's laddish anecdote, we could ask what sort of "message from others" might push middle age, contemplating its dead youth, to try to reanimate its old glamour? To cite in reply, "the message of the cultural imperative to be beautiful" seems too imprecise, unhelpfully broad. Yet something of a similar breadth—the idea of the self formed not quite by, but across, a social message—is a conviction pursued by some philosophers of identification, for whom the psychology of individuation is inherently dislocating. Individuation runs across people, rather than emerging from them.[37] A subject is formed through its withdrawal; and they imply that identification's affect is only uncertainly social, in that it cuts across people rather than either emanating from within them, or herding them together.

Here is a point at which the erratically social nature of identification and the syntax of retrospect start to chime with each other. It is, after all, our bodies which are constant live bridges for us between the external and internal. Someone's concession to his once having seemed beautiful throws open a hinge onto a dizzying space of attributions to others, a space thronged by watching eyes; but exactly *as* the verbal embodiment of this vertiginous space, which is also the space of words, the linguistic-psychic discourse of agreeing to have been what he was in others' eyes does perfectly well. For the little vanity of such retrospective identification is always social, even when it is muttered secretly to itself under its breath. It has no choice but to invent and evoke the authority of others, in order to found its own being. "But, my dears, you should have seen me when I was young!"—such camp announcements are emphatically social acts, or acts of resocialization. Usually, though, these confessions are not voiced. Modesty forbids them; and modesty, because of its reserve, is never weak. What we confide to ourselves under our breath usually overwhelms any louder confession. It is a murmuring conversation with ourselves, to whom we usually chatter in other clichés and shorthand anyway. Our inner speech compulsively mimics what it has overheard. It tends not to run to originality. But actually there is nothing so private about it, save in its literal inaudibility; the "inner voice" is something largely fetched home from the outside. So the inner voicing of our lost looks might serve as an illustration of what Volosinov called a psychic-ideological compound; a piece of talk coming from the outside world, imported inside and fully at home there.[38]

"What I want back is what I was" is, then, less of a whispered script for solitary preening before the mirror than it first appears. In its determined naïveté, it reaches for an impossible wholeness, achieved through a paradoxical retrieval which traces its dissolution into the far past. Even (or, as I've come to think, especially) with this banal example of a small familiar vanity, we are in the larger air of any identificatory moment which lays claim to have discovered what it is now through its compelling onrush of feeling what it was then. This is close to what Joan Scott, writing about retrospective identifications in nineteenth-century history (with regard to feminism's periodic embrace of a glowing and maternalist unity of "women"), has termed the phenomenon of the "fantasy echo" whereby "echo is not so much a symptom of the empty, illusory nature of otherness as it is a reminder of the temporal inexactness of fantasy's condensations, condensations that nonetheless work to conceal or minimize differences through repetition."[39] Indeed from this perspective, the florid instance of "false memory syndrome" is not at all far from the strange syntax of mourned beauty.

The peculiar recalcitrance of beauty, which, lost, can't quite be made to parallel other losses, is mirrored in the strange temporality of its mislaying and refinding. Though what does it really matter, this general and mildly perverse lament that now we no longer have something which we never really had then? And isn't this anyway just the usual means by which, according to Hegel, the universal is realized: through the retrospective retrieval of the particular?[40] Or, dully, aren't such ordinary habits of private, even furtive efforts at consoling ourselves the trivia on which, in the face of the real griefs of the world, we shouldn't waste time? Yet the grand collective designations of nation, ethnicity, religion—these identifications which do operate as often devastating counters in the political world—are arguably reliant on the selfsame mechanisms of retrospective identification, on similar elements of submission and of complicit consent to interpellation, on the same saturation in fantasy. But in the case of our lament for our lost looks, so evident in the flourishing of the beautification economies, there is a departure: here no exhilarated fresh selves can appear to rediscover their communality arising from their subjugation. Unless a real belief is held in the resurrection of the body, good as new, there is no hope here of redemption through the assertion of some common identity. We—the godless ones, anyway—know our fate. So I don't want to advance this instance of artificially recalled beauty as a neat prototype of what happens, only magnified, in the historical growth of the larger identifications. Nevertheless, through my frivolous-sounding example of the ordinary mourning of extinguished beauty, the prominence is highlighted of the common formula: how we can now settle to become what we (think we) were told then. So is that other critical note of vicarious consent: "So this is how I must have been seen by them, but only now do I realize they were right." What a study of the language of lost looks can offer to a broader account of self-designation—of why people classify themselves—is this element of secretive assent to what "they" said once. Such recall may well be an invention, but its historical accuracy or otherwise is beside the point of understanding how this grammar of retrospective retrieval operates.

There are blind spots in language which are not flaws but are constitutive of it, needed for its workings. One of these is the fact that I must speak and hear, as I live, from within the blinkers of the first person pronoun. Our inability to see ourselves as others see us has its equivalent in words; we do not speak or hear ourselves quite as others speak or hear us, and there results a great deal of imaginative effort, second-guessing, empathetic misinterpretation, and gross misattribution. It is in this necessary endemic blindness that the virtue of the cliché appears. And the plaints I've sketched here are clichés of feeling. Their tone is formulaic, sentimental, complacent, swathed in the nostalgia emerging from envisaging ourselves as we once were, in an effort driven by our will to be flattered. As descriptions of how we their speakers actually were, their truth value is at best shaky. But these ordinary quiet utterances are, above all, *linguistic structures of feeling.*[41] As such, their effectiveness stems from their apparent weaknesses, their bagginess and their porosity; it's these which allow them to be open to everyone. Through their looseness their usefulness emerges, in the inelegance which will actually "speak volumes" in fostering the ability of the merely implied to become the perfectly understood, and in admitting the deep intelligibility of the not-said.

Among these linguistic structures of feeling, vanity's habitual loneliness tries to console and fortify itself by appealing to itself as glimpsed from the outside. How many other kinds of identification depend on a similar tacit urge to consolation built on the uneasy supposition that since we can't be certain of being or of having it in the present, then we must have been it or must have had it in the past? To make quite sure of this supposition, though, we'll need to recall, or to invent, the witness of others. It's as if we feel ourselves to have contrived to become human, to have managed to be "like everybody else" only in retrospect—which means, only through a very ordinary linguistic fantasy of retrospect, an elastic thing. If other sorts of identification are sustained through a syntax of compensation and consolation, this would account for a good part of their impassioned tenacity.

THREE

The Right to Be Lonely

*

How single is single? Is One the founding start of a series—or is it an atom? There could be two broad tactics in the movements toward new family forms: to cope with the furious miseries of social exclusion by the gesture of nominating absolutely everyone as a legitimate family (and could a family of one also be ushered into this all-embracing kinship?), while an opposing gesture might declare that really no one constitutes a family, but then no-one should want to, anyway. In the teeth of the former tendency to incorporate more and more contenders into the realm of the familial (with which "the social" is increasingly and fatally taken to be coterminous) I offer instead the wilful principle of The Right to Be Lonely. As oxymoronic as many another claim to rights, my theatrical slogan will be embellished with remarks about the immediately emotional metaphoricity—a metaphoricity not separable from, but sunk in, social realism—of all talk about societal "exclusion" and "inclusion," about outsiders and insiders.

"The right to be lonely" is both a consoling defense that will not work, and a parody. It enacts the vacancy of claims to rights which repose triumphantly on the authority of their own assertiveness, and by inversion it also parodies the plaintiveness of a felt exclusion. (But this slogan is not, of course, intended to advocate "having one's own space" as a gleaming lifestyle, in the name of some repellent and impossible autonomy. Nor do I proffer it as any romanticization of loneliness—which must, if episodically or without acknowledgment, be everyone's common enough fate.) Still, this right to be lonely may serve to interrogate the diction of belonging. For do we unequivocally *want* this social inclusion? Certainly we may want to speak for equality, but in doing so, to steer clear of its now usual accompaniment of a treacly talk of belonging, spiritual recognition, and community. Can it be avoided? Probably not. Does any rhetorical "we" (like this use of it I make now) rely on it? Yes. But the impulse to inclusion also runs a circuit of envy in all agitation about who and what is in, and who and what is not. With such jealousy any drive for greater social inclusion is as driven as any society gossip column—while one unhappy by-product of striving for enlarged acceptability is to push the resulting residue of everyone else further into the backwoods of an unspeakable deviancy. This, ironically, is a concomitant of promoting new family forms. No one is to blame for it.

It is pragmatically necessary to fight for what's sometimes termed the *legitimation* of unorthodox lives; yet this may be best done in the bitter knowledge that through this process, new hierarchies of social acceptability are being generated. Then what are the emotional limits to this thing called legitimation or recognition? If, for instance, you cannot have certain rights on the death of your lover, where that person is of the same sex as you, you might indeed be passionately concerned to gain legal recognition for your liaison. Yet if you are a long-established mistress, or the male lover of a married man, you too are standardly excluded, so as not to increase the distress of the wife and children: isn't this a social exclusion which you would find painfully acceptable? (A strict etiquette, certainly more bourgeois than the bourgeois, for the conduct of such affairs could well prove less damaging than the usual fight of the romantic against the familial, which only sets this antagonistic pair in stone and makes everyone unhappy: and a part of this etiquette would entail knowing when one is properly displaced.) We also suffer greatly from the deaths of our friends, to whom we can have no state-sanctioned recognition. Our sorrow is sharpened by whatever form of neglect it happens to have at hand to feed it, but only in some circumstances do we interpret official nonrecognition as a cruel social exclusion. For this ambiguous state of affairs, we might also reproach our wavering discourse of "public" and "private" itself, a language which also, unevenly, speaks us. Language is hot, and language is historical.[1] It drags along or cajoles lives with it. There is an emotive topography in that spatial conceptualization of inclusion and exclusion itself; it is this linguistic emotionality which suffuses all political philosophies of who is in and who is left out.[2]

Concepts are often constructed in a language which is quietly figurative. In the frequent spatiality of conceptual thought, a fundamental metaphoricity of place and depth is embedded (as in those very words *residual, fundamental, embedded*).[3] But is such an observation merely a rebirth of old fevers of the excessively literalized etymological radicalism which gripped many wild nineteenth-century linguists?[4] For one soon becomes unsure of whether such "layers" of thought's organization are to be considered figurative or not—while to depict these topographies would demand a historian of extraordinary balance.[5] Then if the names of the structures of thought are themselves metaphorical, isn't the very idea of their being any "structure" to thought itself also figurative?[6] Yet if so, what would constitute the nonfigurative here? Such doubts typically rise through the muffled half silences of dead metaphor. Because one cannot extract oneself from it, this blurs the edges between what counts as metaphor and what as literal to that point of fascination where the seemingly literal has its presumption of nonmetaphoricity abruptly drained out of it. There is an area, almost unnameable, where metaphorical description bleeds into the nonmetaphorical. Or there is a lonely hour, which never quite arrives, of the nonmetaphoricity of language.[7] Concepts, often figurative, are mapped onto each other, working in tandem "within the unity of the verbally constituted consciousness," as Volosinov put it.[8] Yet what if the very concepts which ground this overlapped consciousness, those of an external world and an internal world, begin themselves to ring strangely in our ears; what if all this interiority and its opposing exteriority are also themselves metaphorical? And then the ensuing question relentlessly becomes: metaphorical to what?

So we lurch on already-unsteady ground when we scrutinize the public/private distinction and its relative, the social/personal, since from one angle these are particular and mutable historical and sociological renditions of the fundamental and vexed outer/inner division.[9] There is a long history of worry about the volatile meanings of the social itself, which is arguably periodically sexed. Jacques Donzelot's comment here is exemplary—"How did we pass from a usage of 'the social' understood as the problem of poverty, the problem of others, to its current definition in terms of a general solidarity and the production of a life-style: what enabled it to be made into a showcase of development, whose defence comes before all else, something to be offered to the world at whatever cost?"[10] One answer turns on how the self is imagined to be distributed—whether it is torn and reallocated as aspects of the social, or is kept as one thing, set over and against the social.[11] If we hold that the conception of social space is itself metaphorical, as there is not literally a great exterior which stands massively against our separate interiorities, it may be somewhat easier to disentangle that problem of the self's "passage" outward and across into the social, since instead one can claim to be already social. Then the puzzle of passing between these realms, of transferring between them, need not arise with all its attendant apparatus of the dialectic of social outer and psychological inner. For we are outside from the start.[12]

That resolution tout court, though, may be too breezy. Convictions of our interiority well up again, constantly. Perhaps that founding spatiality in thought, beyond which it seems impossible to reach, is partly based on our embodied senses, according to which, for instance, words do rise inwardly to pass outward through our lips.[13] Yet, and especially if we take the thought of the body and what lies beyond its skin as founding perception, there is no commensurate equivalence of outer and inner, and as Gaston Bachelard warns, "it must be noted that the two terms 'outside' and 'inside' pose problems of metaphysical anthropology that are not symmetrical."[14] Then doesn't the usual inner/outer or private/public bifurcation have an element of fantasy in its symmetry—a fantasied regularity? If we then transpose this misleading neatness of these broad figurative pairings to a local variant, the couple of the social and the presocial seems romantically misconceived in its division. There is an unspeakable outside, an imagined asocial space, where something howls beyond the edges, prowls in anguish around the dark perimeter encircling the glowing campfire of the family. If, gripped by this image, we merely enlarge the scope of the family circle and see off a few truly recalcitrant hyenas to the outer blackness, then we have glossed over interesting difficulties. There is a strong argument for rejecting this imagined lure of the thought of the wild outside versus the regulated familial inside. It is the lure of the tame which may best render strange the familiar. Against the tidily paired antitheses are quite other conceptualizations which run right across them, whether from the side of the feminisms which have insisted on the imbrication of the political with the personal, or from other traditions which have emphasized the enunciative weight of public language to work within the sites of intimacy, whether as creator of the subject, or as a rude encroachment: "Things have come to a pretty pass when religion is allowed to invade the sphere of private life," as Lord Melbourne remarked on hearing an evangelical sermon.[15] Exteriority set against interiority surfaces, too, in questions of where the truth of the self is better located; here the standard private-public opposition cannot begin to hold, because language goes with us into the house. We are shaped in speech so as to make nonsense of any of the usual contrasts of domain.[16] Language is already waiting in the house, too; and "the private" is neither the play of liberating anarchic abandon, nor captured by a social control which stalks each bedroom. Rather there are constantly regenerated, audibly argued accounts as to what counts as and what constitutes this private.

If, as so many ways of thinking have intimated, there is a truth of ambivalence, then there are mutual instabilities of inner and outer, an innocent *ekstasis* of language, a propulsion of the unconscious from the outside, and an uneven mutability of public and private. All that is in contrast to the supposition that the public/social is a potentially generous ground for future harmony, or conversely that the social remains a realm of sheer coercion. It is true that the concept of ambivalence cannot be readily translated into a good. And if from the side of optimism "Man is half-open being,"[17] there is also a great deal of slamming shut to be heard. It's not, though, helpful to retreat to the certainties of what I decide is closed to me, to suppose that I am condemned to try to insinuate my small way into some swollen place of the social that has shut me out. Spatial metaphor's ready linguistic affect may imply that I am the private and enfeebled inner, while the vast outside of the social is the terrain of my coming emancipation. But then I cannot wait around too long for my inclusion there, since whatever is social has, like me, only a limited lease on life and is eroded by the brute passage of time. However, if ideas of temporality supplement the achronology of topographical metaphor, then such changes can be understood less devastatingly, as in Hegel's writings on the family as the natural form of ethical life, which passes in its division into civil society. At one point he meditated on the fact that as children grow up "separated from their source—a separation in which the source dries up,"[18] so their parents naturally fall away from their joint incarnation in their offspring and, altered by time, are disaggregated into their separate lives again. This is why Hegel's family, despite its thesis of eventual regeneration in disintegration, was tersely annotated by J. N. Findlay thus: "It is concerned with individuality raised out of the unrest and change of life into the universality of death, ie the Family exists to promote the cult of the dead."[19] Indeed death as our common prospect—rather than any pulsating communality of life—may be more darkly viewed as what truly underlies all visions of social cohesion, as with John Donne's "No man is an island, entire of its self. Every man is a piece of the continent, a part of the main: if a clod of earth be washed away by the sea, Europe is the less as well as if a promontory were; . . . any man's death diminishes me, because I am involved in mankind: And therefore never send to know for whom the bell tolls. It tolls for thee."[20] This celebrated quotation flashes from collectivity straight to its justification as private death. Its sociality is that of our common steady journey from swaddling clothes to winding sheet. I am diminished by any dying which in its bleakly democratic guarantee might as well be, and some day assuredly will be, my own. This communality of death as shared fate returns me forcefully to myself, since "timor mortis conturbat me." Fearful apprehension of death disquiets me—it disturbs me, no longer us. It drives us into our terminally atomized selves; as particles we regain our singularity, our subjection to judgment, and our hope of resurrection. Then the urgency of timor mortis may sharpen envy's hurry to attain incorporation in the social mass before my death. There are others I must win through to, now. Here this question again becomes pressing: "But who are these others who form the outside in relation to this inside which we believe ourselves to be?"[21]

I am not inside anything. I'm not outside it, either. Yet the public/private distinction, which has such solid realities in its effects, tends in its topographical conceptualization to underwrite the affective metaphoricity of inner and outer. This cuts many ways. I look on from outside at something "social" I want to penetrate, as if its secrets are withheld from me. Or, as if inexorably caught inside, I gaze dreamily outward. I may long to break out of my private cell and into the buoyant air of the wide world, yet may also long to diminish this public space by cracking its secrets to ensure that it withholds nothing from my prying. I need the outside to fulfill its promise of largesse to me, I need to master it as my territory: so I cut it down to size, and its promises, viewed close up, may offer me only disappointment and intensify my persistent drive to compel it to reveal yet more of its receding interiority.[22] Whichever way the movement across the imagined membrane which separates the inner and the outer, it is envious and full of pathos. In such discursive spatiality there is, immediately, an affective topography of being excluded: you are where I myself would prefer to be: that is what I would like to have. "So that is marriage, Lily thought, a man and a woman looking at a girl throwing a ball."[23] In this neatest of sentences, which holds so many pairs of eyes, we glimpse in a flash the meditative watcher who herself looks on at a couple who are conjoined as such through their contemplation of the child playing. And perhaps just such a "looking on" might constitute more or less everyone's relation to the family, irrespective of whether they actually inhabit one. Suppose that the ideal of a proper familial life resists me, is something that I feel that others have, yet I lack? Even if I can offer some reasonable approximation to it, I do not have it in the same way that I imagine others having theirs. Not only because I may have failed to quite amass the correct ingredients (maybe I lack a father here, a cousin there, am rather short of ancestors) but because that thing the Family will, in its terrible iconicity, exceed my capture of it. This is all quite irrespective of the actual configurations of people I live with; the family may be something that by definition everyone else but me is felt to have. The commandment in the King James Bible "Thou shalt not covet thy neighbour's house, thou shalt not covet thy neighbour's wife nor his manservant nor his maidservant, nor his ox, nor his ass, nor any thing that is thy neighbour's"[24] isn't so much an instance of bathos as, in its intermingling of a consumerism of desire with a consumerism of household chattels, of the homogenizing logic of envy. Envy is a great maker of lists. It is sharply indifferent, as the commandment recognizes, to any hierarchies among goods, since it reduces everything alike to that which cannot be enjoyed by me—while it is itself greatly energized by the entire diction of public or private boundaries.

That diction changes under our noses, often unforeseeably. Speaking now, and sheepishly, in the first person as a serial single parent, I found consolation in the arrival in the 1990s social policy vocabulary of a new entity, the "single parent *family*" with its formally depathologizing noun—as if this had at last let me detach myself from pressing my nose flat against the glass of the familial shop window and be ushered inside, tolerated now as nothing more noxious than a variation on a norm, rather than as it had been; as an antagonistic thing, a failure in the light of the one true family form.[25] (My relief was strong once I'd grasped how the language of permissible family structures had expanded through the three decades I'd been living them; whereas my children, being of another generation, seem never to have doubted their standing as a family.) Nevertheless, this liberalized talk in some quarters of British life was accompanied by wider kinds of denigration, repathologizing measures, and a welfare regime which is the least generous in western Europe to single parents, even as their numbers increase. But beyond this, I'm also suspicious of my happy relief in my newfound capacity to count as a family. What is the longing to be a family *too* (beyond the prudent wish to be recognized as a social unit which is treated in law accordingly), a longing which is not merely practical but resembles a search for some anchorage; as if the bonds of friendship, often more enduring than the bonds of marriage, are not enough and as if the stronger affinities must always be felt to run downward to our descendants, not laterally? Why do "we all" want to be seen as a family—if indeed "we" do? To be socially recognized also means to be tabulated, monitored, and regulated. As the psychoanalyst Moustapha Safouan remarked apropos recent liberalizing changes in French family law: "The more they ask for liberty, the more they ask for laws."[26] This surface paradox is also all too comprehensible, and liberty has sound reasons for looking to its own policemen. But it will also be patrolled by checks it does not entirely care for. It will also generate fresh kinds of competition between forms of supposed social deviance to see which can attain greater respectability; so if the more parents and the more money the better for a child, then to possess two homosexual parents should be judged a better fate than to own only one, of any kind.[27] Any "stable" couple, irrespective of the sexes of those who constitute it, promise the financial and emotional respectability of a joint household against the assumption of transient entanglements for the single mother and her lesser capacity to earn, offering her only the faintest of prospects of achieving what the paterfamilias Gomez Addams calls "the indescribable joy of having children, and of paying someone else to raise them."[28] If the present expansion of the definition of a family is largely benign as it frays the stiff bonds of the old order, there's also the fact that any increased liberalization of speech, of law, and of culture — without an increased liberalization in the distribution of economic resources — will generate new material inequalities of its own. Meanwhile the new reproductive technologies lend themselves to private arrangements which will tend to outpace legal regulation because of their sheer speed of development; while any childbearing, for those who can regulate it, will increasingly become a matter of affordability. All this change happens in an enlarged societal realm which, expanded by recently recognized familial ties, pushes back the margins to swell and puff up the sphere of the social, until only the thinnest fringe of an unutterably dreadful asociality skirts it. Then is every utopia to be encircled by a dystopia? No doubt: it shouldn't surprise us to find that liberalizing moves also produce fresh forms of the socially inadmissible. Then demands for family equality and nondiscrimination should, ideally, be voiced without being couched in a rhetoric of competing virtue, higher claim. Yet such a rhetoric may well prove strategically indispensable; if only one could avoid believing that such strategies are anything more — or equally important, anything less — than strategical.

The "traditional" family's demise is coinciding with a furious intensification of its variants.[29] It is the fate of the newer contenders to familialism to need to be seen to be doing it not simply as well but better than the older, as women have long observed of their migrations into traditionally male work. The anomalous family must mimic the virtues supposedly enacted within the conventional family form, and be seen to outshine it.[30] In any event, it's as if one must count as a family in order to count at all; while the numbers of those living alone, across western Europe at least, rise sharply. Yet as households of single people grow, the admission of even occasional loneliness remains taboo, while to be without visible social ties is inexcusable. Such common solitariness may be willed and decidedly preferred by its bearer, or it may barely be tolerated, enforced: yet a taint of vice always clouds it. (In 1757, Diderot sent Rousseau his play *The Natural Son*, whence umbrage was taken: "In reading it, Rousseau came upon Constance's words 'Only the wicked man lives alone' and was instantly convinced that the remark was aimed at himself.")[31] And does to live alone render a woman not only wicked, but desexed; need everyone be descriptively drawn into the meshes of the social, especially women, as if these owned a naturally greater emotional extensionality, had more tentacles? The right to be lonely could also suggest the prospect of being alone yet being understood as also social within one's solitariness. Solitude, as a pretty noun often religiously linked to creativity's desiderata, may be acknowledged to be necessary; this admission is anodyne enough. But there's a stronger solitude which refuses to be understood as merely presocial and which rejects the benevolent will to make everything, and it too, familial. This solitude has no time for any plangency about its own "exclusion." Indeed, it groans at the prospect of being tenderly ushered into the domain of the new social; its bearers are in no constellation but live as units of one, are maybe childless, parentless, without siblings, unattached, unmarried, widowed, are not communitarian, are transiently or are even (they can't know) permanently single, and are not in a panic. They simply find themselves alone. The question "how single is single" could ask: how might such singleness neither be considered pathological nor be swept up, in an ostentatious depathologizing, into a compulsive sociability? While her impulse to attain warmth by responding to that imperative familial call is not to be scorned, the figure of the Solitary might yet be retrieved, and in terms other than her failure to attain to the family. Might a properly recognized state of singleness (to wrench the notion of "recognition" away from its usual oppressively gregarious tone) recast that desolate and resentment-prone metaphoricity of social exclusion—and might it also somewhat allay the burden, or at least the embarrassed self-reproach, of those who may find themselves effectively living in solitude at the very same time as they live inside the family?

FOUR

Some WHYs and *why mes*

*

WHY

Children are murdered; and among the heaps of cellophane-wrapped
bouquets, teddy bears, and handwritten verses, cards regularly appear
tied to the wilting flowers with the word WHY written on them, often in
capitals and in felt tip, sometimes with a question mark but often without, as if hopelessness had flattened out any searching interrogation into
a blank statement. Such cards have become part of today's panoply of
public mourning, the garnish of funerals and memorial services, passive
as any laid wreath. They are new rituals, especially of that vicarious — or
vulturous — kind of mourning where the sorrows of the bereaved parents
of the murdered daughters are described as those of "the community"
or even of the nation.

Visiting the site of death, you lay down the written word WHY as tenderly as you lay down your bunch of bright carnations swathed in cello-
phane. The word on the card itself becomes a deposition, a funeral gesture placed among the others which have ousted the wearing of black
armbands. Yet this WHY, a prostrated inert thing, is also a provocation.
To whom is it put? The writers of such cards will realize perfectly well that
the only answer to their implied "Why was this innocent life destroyed?"
is swift and brutal-sounding: that here there is no *why* to be answered
other than by a terse *because*. And that the selection of the victim was arbitrary, just another case of "being in the wrong place at the wrong time."
Or, if their single scrawled WHY is taken as an appalled but genuine in-

quiry about the state of the killer's mind, or of the terrible world in which killers can go about their business, then the writers of WHY realize that no passing reader is going to answer them, while to begin to shape their own reasons, they'd need to embark on prolonged arduous studies in the criminology of deviance, psychopathology, or theology. Today's familiar Christian answer to them is that God is there, present at the heart of the most terrible of situations, even though from our limited point of view He is not apparent as an actor. Yet you wouldn't bother to write WHY if you believed this. And faith, anyway, should not interrogate its Maker in this way; if a lengthy essay of explanation, signed God, were to appear overnight among the fading bouquets, that would indeed be disquieting and for more than one reason. Nevertheless, who else is your WHY addressed to, if it's not an appeal to God to grant us, at the least, more illuminating television theologians. Perhaps in this WHY there is some seriously searching hope for enlightenment; perhaps there is the ghost of some doctrinal anguish. Or it could hold a positively complacent satisfaction in the tacit admission that the heavens won't ever reply to the word tacked onto the funeral flowers. It is one of the class of why expressions expecting nothing, like any Latin question preceded by num which signals its coming answer "No"; indeed the WHY on the bunch of carnations could only expect the divine response to be, Oh, bugger off!

This WHY (them?) is, fortunately, a specialized and rarely provoked occurrence. An ordinary plaint is the Why (me?) of the sufferer, the victim of circumstances, of illness. Closest among the fertile tangles of rhetorical classification to epiplexis (the posing of questions in order to reproach, grieve, or inveigh), the summation of "Why me?" is Job's lament "Why died I not from the womb? why did I not give up the ghost when I came out of the belly?"[1] Voluble Job was upbraided for his talk by one of his unhelpful comforters, confident that he recognized a rhetorical question when he heard one: "How long wilt thou speak these things? and how long shall the words of thy mouth be like a strong wind?"[2] Like a strong wind, that is; not like a request for information. Suppose a why like Job's is largely a complaint, then is it even a question, if it isn't really asking anyone anything? There's a dull if economical answer: everyone understands that these are only rhetorical questions which by definition don't expect any reply. Yet are such lamenting whys real examples of that genre, though? *Erotema*, rhetorical inquiries, ought to carry a spirit of willed indifference to any actual answer. Convinced in advance of what the response should be, they aim only to affirm their point by framing it as a question. Nevertheless even the most textbook of rhetorical questions, although it may not anticipate or even want any reply, is acutely alert to the presence of its hearer as a sounding board, even if he may be some disappointingly aloof god. Some potentially listening ear of someone or something else, even an echoing rock, is the sole reason for the question to bother to voice itself at all. There need not be any second auditor present, as in the instances where someone acts as her own best listener. Furiously silent addresses to oneself are everyday: "Why the hell am I still struggling here with this unrewarding lonely task?" Questions like this tend to arise only in the small relief of their outburst and in solitude, but others, while also nominally rhetorical, loudly signal the reaction they expect or they even want to induce, even if it's hostile: "How long am I expected to put up with this, then?" There's a marked difference between not wanting an answer, and not needing a listener.

These, though, are broader kinds of rhetorical *whys* than the WHY inscribed by pathos in Why did these children die? (The trouble, though, with pathos is that it becomes unattractive and unpersuasive as soon as its hearers suspect, which is usually very soon, that it knows itself that it's rhetorical. And as for the full form of Why did these innocent children die? the listener could hardly follow its implied invitation to speculate about guilty children and their just deserts.) The difference between such WHYs and the general rhetorical question needing an auditor, but no answer, is that while the plaintive WHYs may understand that no divine voice will boom through a parted cloud with a rationale for this killing or this senseless injury, they do still have their particular question to ask, however hopelessly, of something. But if this something isn't exactly a *who*, then what is it that's addressed by these *why them*, *why me* questions?

why me?

This question looks similar to the mourning ritual Why these children? in that it seems to appeal to natural justice in its absence. It's how people interviewed about their reactions to learning that they have a grave illness often report themselves asking, as if it were an obligatory verbal gesture like the funeral flowers' WHY; "At first I could only wonder, why me? What have I ever done to deserve this?" And such an anxiety about what is or isn't merited also underpins the superficially happier inquiry "Why is it me that you love?" Both these *why mes* of becoming ill and becoming loved are demonstrations of my unease that a critical stage of explanation, the stage which would have shown me my own agency in my fate, has been missed out, with the result that my presence seems arbitrary and violently exposed as naked. A different version of this trope of nakedness is pursued in Bodenheimer's *Warum? Von der Obszönität des Fragens,*[3] which claims that an obscenity is latent in many everyday questions, and this lies in their drive to strip bare the person being questioned and leave them exposed; his analyses range from How are you—alright? to Why are you playing with the pen? Surely, though, the *why me* questions already mentioned here expose the questioner who utters them, and far more than their recipients; and not exactly "obscenely." What is revealed instead is the will of the questioner to be placed at the heart of the event. This impulse to take center stage always falls short of the broader perspective that George Eliot ascribes to her heroine:

> It was not in Dorothea's nature, for longer than the duration of a paroxysm, to sit in the narrow cell of her calamity, in the besotted misery of a consciousness that only sees another's lot as an accident of its own. She began now to live through that yesterday morning deliberately again, forcing herself to dwell on every detail and its possible meaning. Was she alone in that scene? Was it her event only? She forced herself to think of it as bound up with another woman's life—a woman towards whom she had set out with a longing to carry some clearness and comfort into her beclouded youth.[4]

In falling short of this useful question of whose event it is, of where the edges of the event are, so to speak, the *why mes* of illness and love alike lay open their speakers' anxieties, terrors, aggression through their will to secure an unambiguous placing. But what of the special frustrations of the *why me* in, for instance, Why do I have this metastasized cancer? This is a question which is not only, and understandably, self-directed but is also cruelly vulnerable to ephemeral fashions in thinking about health as responsibility. If I have leanings toward the Christian Science which holds that my sickness is the outcome of my false belief, or toward similar convictions that I'm reaping my punishment for my unhealthy lifestyle, or worse, for my old emotional reticence, I'll consider myself to be an agent of my own illness, even if in a spirit of self-reproach. Today an account of disease which can draw its explanations from our newly unearthed genetic inheritance best satisfies this hope for an involvement which is refreshingly guilt free, since we never selected our parents. On the other hand, the specter of an unsuspected genetic legacy as an emerging cause for our children's illnesses must cause us acute guilt. Some *why mes* of disease yearn for an account in which the sufferer has at least a walk-on part, or else, as in Why has my child developed this awful condition?, they long for our exculpation. Either way, pressing questions of how to distinguish between undue guilt and proper responsibility irrupt as these *whys*.

A *why me* typically rushes out in an emergency. Some might argue that then it's really a shout, or a whimper. If so, it also seems a very sophisticated thing, despite its veneer of haplessness, or its frank idiocy which is only sometimes disarming. "Don't be so bloody stupid!" is the reaction it readily gets. Yet its compactness and its overdetermination are admirable. For a *why me* is shorthand for this event has happened and I fear (or hope) I am present in it while simultaneously I fear (or hope) that I am absent. So *why me* boils down to, What's the status of "me" here? or, Where is me? The answer is: Nowhere. The questioner, however, valiantly persists.

To investigate so tenaciously lays us, as questioners, wide open to being investigated ourselves for our very acts of linguistic investigation; Why do you keep asking? What are you really after? If, as the theory of rhetorical questions has it, many a string of words followed by a question mark is not truly a question, the converse also holds. Many an urgent wish to know is never followed by a question mark: "We shan't be meeting again for some time, then." Nevertheless it is an inquiry—which, for reasons of tact or embarrassment, formally conceals itself, leaving its import for its hearer to decipher. True enough, too, that we'll only ask some questions where we are pretty certain in advance of the answer and we want the pleasure of hearing it all over again, but this is a danger-ous game, especially with passion's questions. The most prominent of ostensibly amorous queries can only provoke the disappointment that it nervously anticipates, but also invites. To ask, "Do you love me?" is reli-ably catastrophic, and mutually disabling. It issues from the questioner's fearful expectation that the real reply will certainly be No. From the re-spondent's standpoint, only a lie can result where the answer given is Yes—even if that Yes is true.

Still, one obvious rhetorical retort to this anxious *why me*—"Why *not* you?"—is certainly not what the questioner's *Why do you love me?* could ever be relieved to receive. Nor would the sick person be at all diverted to hear "Why *not* you?" For this *why not* is a brusque shorthand: in the nature of things, there is arbitrariness. Put up with it! Why shouldn't it be you who's ill? This is why the apprehensive lover who has asked, "Why me, why do you want me?" wouldn't be greatly reassured to have "But why *not* you?" flung lightly back at her, since it makes one truth clear; that lovers are interchangeable, that it's contingency which is determining, that while she is perfectly good as a candidate for the job, one object of passion might perfectly well have been another, and doubtless soon will be. Yet at least she is returned, or rather she is elevated by, this "Why *not* you?" to membership of the general class of feasible love objects, whose threshold she had previously felt uncertain of attaining—or maybe, to take a cynical view of her question *why me*, she'd privately been hoping to be told she surpassed.

Whatever its genesis, this compulsive *why me* crops up with strik-ing regularity in the lexicon of love's highly automated phrasing. When Lacan remarked that "the function of language is not to inform but to evoke," he explained that it aimed to evoke a response in others.[5] These impassioned *whys*, though, go further. They provoke. They nudge and poke and, in the old meaning of "being provoking," they're vexing and often lead to stalemate. Someone bewildered by his good luck at stumbling into sudden unexpected happiness constantly asks, "But why should you love me, why ever me in particular?" His worldly lover, irri-tated by this bothersome inquiry, almost manages to hide her exaspera-tion from him by quoting "Parce que c'était lui, parce que c'était moi." But this famous saw (its author was Montaigne, writing about his friendship with La Boétie) won't soothe its recipient's disquiet.[6] Montaigne's *parce que* offers a neat fusion of contingency (by implication it might not have been him, or me, it just happened to be) with exactness (this friendship exists precisely because of our particularities in their unique conjuncture). So to the lover's apprehensive question, the *parce que* offers an amiable yet a quite threateningly unsatisfactory answer when it explains "It's all because of the fact of you with me; aligned, we make up something particular." For his *why me* puzzle is sharpened by his strong suspicion that perhaps we're not at all particular one to the other, we're perfectly arbitrary and interchangeable, and indeed he himself may be highly disposable in his present scenario of love. He had really wanted to incite some reply which drew on something stronger and warmer than the elegant contiguity of "Parce que c'était lui, parce que c'était moi." Serendipity is not enough for the lover, who demands necessity.

His fretfulness readily lends itself to an easy inversion: so Roland Barthes can declare, "Even as he obsessively asks himself why he is not loved, the amorous subject lives in the belief that the loved object does love him, but does not tell him so."[7] But I think we could plausibly twist Barthes's formulation and instead say, there is also the Why *do* you love me? which fears that it is not loved at all. Whatever the emotional truth of this may be, we can be reasonably confident that the situational truth of this *why me?* is only raised where its speaker longs to feel herself somehow, even tenuously, involved in having brought about some heavily charged state. So I really do need my Why do you love me? to provoke some reply, even as I intuit that it must disable the person it's put to. At worst I must answer it myself. (And the only way I'd ever get the longed-for response would be through this kind of furtive inner dialogue: "Why me as your choice of love object?—Because I am terribly desirable, *that's* why, and it took a person of your rare discernment to appreciate this.") A familiar variation on this theme is the beseeching plea "But what do you see in me?" This can be answered helpfully only with "Nothing." To be told that something is seen in me would do me no service. For then I'd have been turned into a wrapping around some delicious nugget of qualities to which I remained insensible myself and to which I could enjoy no access; whereas my question "What do you see in me?" had really longed to be told about my own pertinence to my being loved, but in a way I, too, could grasp. My question is a hope for some presence of my own in my fate, of a kind to credit me with at least some response-inducing qualities. Otherwise I'm exposed as frail in the face of contingency. Which in fact I am.

If these emotive *why mes* are voiced from their speaker's frustrated wish to have a bearing on her destiny which is intelligible to her, they're condemned to arise too late, after the event. The thing already appears as sealed. Not just murder or grave illness but mundane daily life, too, enforces a pugnacious retrospect by delivering you its *Because* like a punch on the nose, and then leaving you struggling to put your faint *Why* to it afterward. So typically enough, as the object of a trivial and casual attack on a London street my first reaction was to exclaim, flustered and stupefied, to a passerby, "But *why*? I wasn't doing anything to them, you saw I was just quietly walking along, I wasn't bothering those boys in any way." An unreflecting impulse in this instant reaction of *why me* wants both to have been anonymous and therefore unassailably innocent, yet also to have been present as yourself, to have counted for something in that scene where in fact *you* were not, only your shell was present, the middle-aged woman's shell, the whole small affair a dreadful witness to what you'd already thoroughly understood: that when someone glimpses you they don't see any "essential you," they simply see a shape, and in this street incident an unremarkable unathletic shape unlikely to go in hot pursuit of them. My autopilot *why* had briefly forgotten this, in the shock of collision; the longing to be innocent (a fact of which it's perennially hard to be confident) in an event without reason, colliding with the wanting some reason there, in order for me to be a factor within it.

This was impersonal bad luck. A piece of impersonal good luck, though, doesn't usually arouse any such a *why me?* Logically, it should. If after decades of lying dormant, my old lottery ticket unexpectedly wins me a tenner, I don't bother to ask *why me*, or even Why haven't I had a win long before now? I pocket the cash as if it's only my due. Why *not* me? anticipates its own luck. Much buying of lottery tickets must be inspired by a quiet conviction that although I know that I've a one in several million chance of winning, at the same time it feels to me that my doing so with this ticket is equally as likely as not. Taking any kind of gamble, I'll naturally divide my future into the two outcomes: my winning, or not winning. And this alternative sounds like a fifty-fifty proposition. It's as if each single stake has an equally good chance of winning against any other, and in the boundless democracy of hazard, my pound's tiny worth is as good a candidate for fortune as any other; so why *not* me?

But a different *why me* of achieved good fortune, the "Why is it me you love?" resembles a small explosion in a deep gulf. In this it's strikingly akin to the *why me* of misfortune. The gulf, seemingly quite unbridgeable, lies between my wish to have had an effective presence in the event so that it will carry traces of my will, my characteristics, or my actions in it—and my recognition, which I cannot evade for long, of sheer accident, contingency. I'm called on to bear the fact that at the same instant I'm in the picture and out of it. My *why me?* starts wildly forward in this clash of realizing that what's happened has something to do with me although not in a way that I can help, while at the same time, it has nothing to do with me. I'll try to hold these opposing realizations in my head; out of their lack of congruence leaps a *why me?* This expletive knows that it is me and it isn't me, and it doesn't much like this awareness; it also senses that there is no reconciliation of the two, so it bursts out in the shape of the interrogative that already understands it won't get any answer that will calm it. So after all, this *why me*, both in *why am I loved* and *why was I attacked*, can be returned to the convention of rhetorical questions, in that what's underscored is its own unanswerability—at least in the terms that it wants to hear, and tries its (repeatedly-defeated) best to incite.

WHYS as Questions about Where I Am

The WHY of premature death and the lover's fervent questioning may look, at first sight, like a contrast of disinterested philosophical searching with nervous vanity. But if the *why them* appeals to the sky for illuminating reassurance, whereas the *why me* appeals, even less plausibly, to the lover for it, they do have this in common: they alter interpellation's focus. Its linguistic mechanism has the air of singling me out in its person-targeting impersonality, arguably inducing social formation through guilt.[8] It orders me into the world. But the wish of the *why me* is to be gotten in, to insert itself into events, and establish it there. And while "Why *not* you?" is customarily a tart rejoinder to private invitations wanting reassurance, it can also be provoked where a public rhetorical withdrawal is being made, in the name of progressive politics, from a conservative collectivity. For instance, in Britain the slogan *Not in my name* appeared in its thousands on the posters and banners of marchers opposing attacks on Afghanistan or Iraq. This aimed to expose the illusions of participatory democracy: wage this war as our elected leader, and you act without my consent or the consent of all these others who feel like me—so don't categorize me as a consenting citizen, I'm not what you take me to be. But this *Not in my name* can irritate some fellow marchers, since despite its best intentions, it sounds insufferably pious, as if muttered by a beautiful soul, nervously drawing its skirts away from the dirt and mud of the political world.[9] There's an uncertainty, too, as to the addressee (if any) of *Not in my name*. If it's the hawkish government, then that would remain blithely indifferent to the individual disavowal, but if it's the world in general, there's a fatal overtone of some special discernment on my part, and then the slogan's real address would only be to those who have already understood what I understand. *Not in my name* is a humorless version of a joking paradox: the injunction to "Count me out!" where the count has already enrolled me, so I can only try to cross myself off its list once I'm indelibly registered on it, and where anyway the whole logic of counting is additional, not subtractive: yet at the same stroke, the counter had never counted *me* in, was never interested either in my particularity then, or in my disaffection now. My name just doesn't figure. So the slogan *Not in my name* turns out to share some of the same troubles of the inept inclusion or the premature exclusion of the self which haunt *why mes*. Or is it mistaken to fuss over the nuances of what many must consider an effective slogan of civil disobedience, since they carry it, they sign the petitions and declarations which it heads? Still, Lenin, for one, did not underestimate the importance of tuning slogans precisely to name some new conjuncture and, in that naming, shape it.[10] But then, perhaps *Not in my name* (along with its far preferable variant *Not in our name*) flourishes precisely because it does have that capacity to characterize and infuse the person-centered note of current oppositional politics.

All these various *whys* are stuck with incarnating their askers' dilemmas of wanting to be effective yet also sensing that they are not, that even where they have presence they are still relatively helpless within their presence. Just as a tentative resolution to the unsatisfactory alternatives of speaking language or being spoken by it is to grasp how language may speak across me, so these *why mes* grope toward an idea of presence which neither pulls toward obliterating itself, nor makes any swollen claim to its own efficacy. Both the WHY and the *why me* seek the reassurance of unearthing a guiltless human manifestation in events which are in fact indifferent to them. The guilt of ambiguous agency clasps an inflated responsibility to itself, not solely out of conscientiousness but also out of its less admirable hubris.[11] There's an innocent egotism in all these *whys* of loss and love. This terrible thing has happened to someone else: *why?* I might have been involved somehow, yet I couldn't have been or I'd have stopped it. This terrible thing has happened to me: *why me?* Here I am, in the play of action, yet I'm a pawn. This wonderful thing has happened to someone else: well, *that* seems inevitable. This wonderful thing has happened to me: *why me?* I don't know what I did to earn it—nothing at all that I can see, so I'll probably lose it. In short, these *why mes* are conspicuously lacking in irony. Still, the most transparently neurotic of questions may work as a powerful strategy; but more interestingly, we can consider why anyone would *want* to ask them—what a sense of one's implication in an event would secure, that a conviction of one's irrelevance would destroy.

Why have these *whys* and the *why mes* drifted from their real dilemmas of oscillating emphases of moral questions ("I must be involved in this somewhere" vying with "I am not responsible for this") to acting as metaphysical interrogatives; why their displacement behavior in posing rhetorical questions? Hard to state an excluded middle; difficult to balance inside a pressing thought and not tilt and collapse onto one side or another, either the self-importance of guilt or the insouciance of self-exoneration. Still, these stubborn questions are plainly intelligible in use. We appeal through them, maneuver with them, steer around them without much difficulty. "The question is not one of explaining a language-game by means of our experiences, but of noting a language-game."[12] It isn't a matter of deciphering what the perpetrators (us) of these maddening *why mes* would *really* be revealed to be asking, if only we could therapeutically analyze them with acute enough discernment or crack open their hermeneutic disguise. It's more a matter of registering that our commonest *whys* are working as forms of language saturated in strong affect—are working directly, without apology or veiling. And because of that immediacy, they won't be satisfied by any answering "because," which, lured by the *why mes'* overt semantic content, overlooks their ardor of utterance itself.

FIVE

Linguistic Inhibition as a Cause of Pregnancy

*

The word is indeed made flesh and dwells amongst us. But sometimes, too, it's the absence of the word which results in the making of yet more flesh. What is *not* said can have solidly physical repercussions. A child can be a consequence of verbal inhibition. Yet there are reasons for this which are more engaging than (for here others' harsh judgments rush unhesitatingly in) the stupidity, or the prudishness, so easily ascribed to its parent. For it takes a tough composure to manage what's involved: to make yourself, within a scenario which ideally has dissolved all separateness, speak instead as a thing to a thing. You might, instead, get pregnant out of politeness. (Which doesn't, in itself, commit you to damning either condition.)

Linguistic Inhibition and Linguistic Distraction

Suppose that language in use embodies emotions proper to it: there is linguistic love; there is linguistic feeling which rises sharply as loaded utterance; there is linguistic repletion; there is pleasure in poetic exactingness. But there's certainly linguistic dread in articulation, too; stammering apprehensiveness, breathlessness, tremulous unease at even contemplating voicing matters aloud which are hard to broach or may be devastating once out.[1] The darker the likely drama consequent on the telling, the harder to disturb the silence before. The very act of articulation is fraught, for words become weapons even in reluctant mouths. Uttering the charged word is an ejection, as in the hearty instruction to

a reluctant speaker to just "spit it out!" Only by expelling it through pro-
nouncing it can we regain a sense of the loaded word as ordinary speech,
for it becomes unexceptional once it's passed our lips and its thing-like
quality has been transmuted by its movement, for better or worse, out
into the world. It's a linguistic aggression which the speaker knows she
is about to commit, the aggression of cutting through some settled state.
Her silence then is no thoughtlessness but more often a consequence of
too much thought, too much brooding on how to say it.

Exactly how what's spoken will be received is incalculable, while it
gives rise to feverish calculations in its speaker's head. Some of this anticipation tries vainly to weigh the quiet fringes of words, the trailing
filigree of association which are part of its meaning: "It is the overtone,
halo, or fringe of the word, as spoken in that sentence."[2] The room into
which the sentence itself falls has its own aura of expectations. Each
speech is delivered into its occasion of hearing. The meaning of what's
said bleeds into its unique deployment and the receptivity of its audience, and it becomes them. So does the very act of speaking itself. Some
kinds of articulation ineluctably pull attention to themselves; so with the
linguistic embarrassment of trying a foreign language in which you're
weak, you have to bear being heard, initially, as an odd thing; the same
with owning an unusual voice, a striking regional accent, a lisp, or a
stutter. Self-help manuals advise stutterers to tell strangers at once, "I
stutter. It may take me longer to say a sentence than you are used to."
This tactic aims to restore some mastery of the situation to the afflicted
speaker. Announcing that he knows himself to be a vocal object to others
seizes the authority of reclaiming the accident of his difficulty as his own.
The need to tolerate your speech being heard as a phenomenon, a stare-
inducing curiosity, also arises where getting out an accusation or a public complaint can founder through shyness and reserve. Sufferers from
Tourette's syndrome have it worst; among its tics is compulsive echola-
lia and coprolalia, all verbal restraint destroyed in helpless and explosive
cursing. But, distressing extremes apart, the ordinary delivering of words
is often fraught with the real risk, or the speaker's worried anticipation,
that the very act of articulation will at once dominate what's said.

No wonder, then, that there's so much trembling on the verge of utterance. Yet not speaking is hardly a refuge. A silence can be telling, so much

so that there are moments when you must cut through the thickness of your own silence, just to fill the air with random conversational noise. The pause called pregnant is teeming with its barely restrained impulses to give birth to something irreversible. In the pregnant stillness of anticipation before you break calamitous news, the inner word feels as if it were being moved forward as a waiting thing. It has become an object among objects studded across a massy landscape, a solid block of presence, which you as its coming speaker must heave laboriously into full-throated view. Are its recalcitrance and your effort at dragging it out really no more than an index of your linguistic modesty? Perhaps it's better described as a reluctance to violate an occasion; you long to keep whatever is voiced true in timbre to the whole, but you also realize you can't conceivably control the outcome of your utterance. Poised on the edge of opening her mouth, the speaker here feels herself to be nursing, gingerly, a linguistic grenade. Of its exact force and explosive direction she can't be sure. Hurl it she must, but she too will likely be brought down by it.

To abruptly alter others' anticipation of the sayable would catch its speaker out in a small act of linguistic violence. So her silent embarrassment can retain its stranglehold if she is faced with breaking across what's already been discursively established; to speak then would shatter an expectation. Not necessarily any one person's, but a much broader horizon of expectation, which is powerfully implicit and impersonal. The tendency to preserve the existing mode is strong, and sustained by a hope of understanding and of being understood, not only by the interlocutor of the moment. Inhabiting its tacit etiquette resists changes of register, as if then a chaos of incomprehension would charge in. Linguistic accommodation is an adjustment, half-conscious or automatic, to the verbal mores of others; at the same time, it entails an act of psychological accommodation, of rapid fine-tuning. The more fragile in mood the linguistic situation, the harder it is to go against the habitual impulses of accommodation. Yet to fail to do so can have dire effects. On occasions, a speaker has no option but to turn herself into an instrument of attack, speaking roughly to undo some settled understanding and shove it in another direction. To observe this isn't to plead, by contrast, for better "communication"—something we so often hear extolled, yet which is at best an ambiguous good. For indirection, avoidance, judicious silence, and white lies can be great blessings, and more accurate to their situation. Their enemy, frankness, is often a vice—especially the self-proclaimed kind, which today is the only incarnation of frankness. Nothing makes you flinch faster than a statement prefixed with "To be frank." Hear that, and you know that some sort of sadism is about to be ushered in under the guise of the speaker's admirable manly forthrightness. The same with "Let's be blunt." Not unaffected speech, but the always affected speech of cruelty is guaranteed to follow.

Such plain speaking supposes that its opposite number, linguistic shyness, has caused a fecund proliferation of euphemisms. Its bluntness would despise them both. Yet the exuberantly fertile world of euphemism is actually of little assistance in dissolving anxiety.[3] Shyness wants not to be heard to interrupt. So (with nervously fertile heterosexuality) while mild euphemism could manage to say, "I don't have any form of protection," this would cut across its scene just as surely as its direct version, "I don't want to get pregnant so what kind of contraception do we use?" The study of the ingenious dictionary of euphemism, fascinating in itself, doesn't illuminate the working language of evasion.[4] For evasion, as a discreet version of inhibition, doesn't resort to specific verbal niceties but achieves its more forcefully subtle checks by means of circumlocution. Whereas, despite itself, the use of euphemism always proclaims an unconcealed revelation of the fact of concealment.

Then to be euphemistic is not necessarily to be decorous. Decorum was a fundamental good in the classical lexicon of Rhetoric, where speech had above all to be fitting to its occasion. But at times it needs a chosen blindness to sustain decorum, and it needs a careful refusal of frankness. To pretend not to have heard, to speak as if you had completely failed to notice, can be a kindness. Even if it's often a doubled kindness, which spares its speaker too. True tact not only looks away, but needs to contrive to be seen by its object to have looked away. As in the well-known anecdote of the hotel bellboy who, asked about the difference between politeness and tact, explained it from experience:

> One day I was told to take an armload of fresh towels to one of the bedrooms. So I took them, went there, and knocked. There was no answer, so

I tried the doorknob and found the room unlocked. I thought the guests who'd wanted the towels must have gone out, so I went across the room to leave them in the bathroom. When I opened the bathroom door, there was a woman in the shower. I said quickly, "Excuse me, sir," and I backed out. Now saying "Excuse me" was politeness, but the "sir" part, that was tact.

That is, this bellboy of legend was quick witted and generous enough to lie by putting up the screen of his pretended shortsightedness, or of her invisibility, to shield the sensibility of the naked guest. What's more, he did all this with only a monosyllable.

But usually the word-screens erected in the name of tact are less elegant, and larger. Someone's attempt to wring a badly wanted speech of sentiment out of another usually produces only a resentful or mortified silence, or else an inept distracting barrage of words. The coercion which typically brings on this display of linguistic distraction behavior is to testify to having emotions. If these feelings are owned, they are at once petrified by that very demand. Distraction behavior, as ornithologists call it, is a tactic of some bird species; lapwings and other plovers will act bizarrely in the aim of drawing away some danger to their offspring (for instance, not flying but running off while dragging a seemingly broken wing along the ground, to induce the fox's pursuit). A great deal of uttered language can consist of such a trailing of feathers, much of it no doubt done as instinctively and with as little calculation as the valiant lapwing. But some of it will be done in studied reaction to the perceived threat. Since this line between the practice of evasion and the exercise of tact is so fine, and while myriad opportunities for misconception famously attend sex, the resulting comedies of errors, which always crop up naturally, can readily be engineered as well. The niceties of any lapwing sentence of distraction (such as "Alright, I did tell you I'd fallen in love with you, and that was true, but it didn't mean that I love you, that's a very different thing" or "None of those men you were with in the past could put up with you, so why do you suppose that I should?") might absorb the addressee's attention for months. Eventually she realizes that to have puzzled for so long over their semantic meaning was to have been distracted from the fundamental nature of their utterance, and to have been successfully lured away from the facts by their broken-winged ruse.

Cordelia Cornered

Birds dart purposefully across many of Shakespeare's plays. And their instinctive distraction behavior is also at work in the humans, in the much scrutinized opening scene of *King Lear*.[5] This is more familiarly taken up with, among other matters, eloquence's relationship to sincerity, what good and bad faith in declarativeness is, what verbal chastity is, and what connections may lie between fluency or austerity in utterance, and truth in feeling.

To recap: Goneril's inflated reply to her father's emotional demand appeals to the dull convention that words are inadequate to express great feeling: "Sir, I love you more than words can wield the matter." She declares hers to be "A love that makes breath poor, and speech unable," while, as is always the way with such utterance, she is speaking volubly. At this, the trapped Cordelia mutters to herself, "What shall Cordelia do? Love, and be silent." Having heard Regan's fulsome speech next, she loses heart, but then she recovers it conventionally:

> My love's
> More richer than my tongue.

At first, though, anticipating what will happen, she tries hard to steer clear of any speechifying. Lear: "Speak." Cordelia: "Nothing, my lord." Lear: "Nothing?" Cordelia: "Nothing." Lear: "Nothing will come of nothing. Speak again."[6] Thus father prods daughter into his ritual of statement. When her turn can't be escaped, it's the impossibility of conveying her true feelings in a spoken exhibition that she laments:

> Unhappy that I am, I cannot heave
> My heart into my mouth: I love your majesty
> According to my bond; nor more nor less.

Lear asks about her somewhat legalistic response: "But goes thy heart with this?" To which Cordelia, wretchedly aware that she is on family show, fatally agrees. Later she tells him that she lacks

that glib and oily art
To speak and purpose not.

Cordelia doesn't stay chastely silent. She does speak out, highly reluctantly and in what she realizes is the wrong register for her father's need; in strained position-bound talk, ironically fit for a publicly staged situation. When she declares that she'll love him according to an apt and exact partition of feeling, she cracks the context of Lear's demand and his incitement to her to make ostentatious display. Announcing, instead, the precise measure of her feeling, she's also cramped in the confines of her own rhetoric. For this, stiffly punctilious, is indeed as rhetorical in its truthful exactitude and perverse literalness as were her sisters' cynically mellifluous utterances. Maneuvered into declaration, Cordelia cannot, understandably, oblige with what's sought from her, but she issues rigid talk about the just partition of her loyalties. Hers is exactly the kind of defensively formal response which is produced by the linguistic coercion, which, in its turn, can't be reassured by it. Lapwings run wildly to trail their wings along the ground here. Any question which carries a suspicion of "Just how much do you love me?" is paralyzing to the one questioned. And anything remotely approaching "Say you love me!" can never incite a gratifying answer for the questioner, whatever the real devotion of the respondent. Indeed, the truer here the more mute; or at least the more gauche, as Cordelia shows. Boxed in, she can't dislocate the context of patriarchal demand in order to convey her love, and she can't undercut the bullying public staging of feeling. She ends up with a painful and awkward compromise; the unsuccessful linguistic distraction behavior of her legalese, whose formal accuracy is all too far from the required expressiveness.

Unable to Speak out in Time

But whatever cousinship can there possibly be between Cordelia's thwarted longing to guard her silence under pressure, and the all too successful silence-keeping of the woman who can't in time get out the words "What do we do about contraception?" Only that both of them have realized that to speak out from the immediate place where they find themselves will cause disruption, and by crashing straight through the linguistic expectations of the context. And both of them, like any speaker (although such a training may well be, historically, more deeply inculcated in women) are already practiced in instinctive accommodation to the greater power of an expectant context. Usually this power can be conversationally undermined, nimbly inflected by eel-like evasions, by supple twists aside and off the point, by a studied deafness to what is required, or by the displacements of intricate conversational smokescreens. In an emergency, all this must be exploded.

Cordelia does it one way. But the woman in bed who is slower to speak (and who, crucially, is afforded no formal moment at which to make her declaration) fails to find another way. I do realize that my example may appear to be written in sepia, in that it predates the morning-after pill, and belongs to a time, a couple of decades ago, when the results of such mutual linguistic ineptness could only be altered by a subsequent abortion. And it predates the advent of AIDS, with its different deployment of "protectives" as barriers against the risk of HIV infection (a change of use which has indeed produced, for some, a whole new erotics of latex). But I cannot dismiss my too-slow woman to the realm of a dubious period charm. And the charm of no periods remains doubtful. It's still the case today that for the awkward heterosexual of any fertile age, any mechanical method of contraception (though here the diaphragm is ambiguous) is prone to the same difficulty in specifying and asking. Whereas the pill allows for silence, concealment, discretion, dissociation—in short, it lets you enjoy your linguistic inhibition but without suffering the consequences. That old and cold instruction "The best contraceptive is the word No!" is undone by the fact that the most effective means of contraception involve no words at all, because it's effected well away from the sexual scene; a pill is swallowed as automatically, privately, and neutrally as teeth are brushed.

Back, instead, to the pre-pill 1940s, where a vignette by Sartre could be read as an early stage in the ultimate scenario of hesitation to name the need for contraception. It exemplifies the same difficulties. His imagined young woman he judges to be in bad faith, because she lets her hand be held by her suitor at the café table, but limply, neither removing it from his grip nor acknowledging his gesture, as if she hadn't registered it. Perhaps she wanted to preserve the moment unshaken by all the laborious emotional acknowledgment and disentangling of feeling which would have ensued; in any event, she draws herself up, says Sartre in a much criticized passage, into high thought and high talk. Later readers might concur that her passivity may not be admirable; but as an act of accommodation, it's hardly so reprehensible as Sartre's diagnosis of bad faith implies.[7] In any event, this Parisian allegory has much in common with our instance of being exposed to the chance of conception, yet hesitating to mention it instantly. Judged from one aspect, there's indeed an element of bad faith here too. Especially if you read it, comically, as if the linguistically inhibited woman's whole body and not just her hand is left lying, without her needed comment. But from another aspect, the Sartrean criticism that bad faith in a complex scenario enacts an artificial self-suspension and self-dissociation can offer us no key to our woman who fails to cry, "Wait!" in time. For hers is not a failure to rise to the real complexity of a situation, in which she acts instead with a misleading simplicity. It is a failure to rise, through any action, to the real simplicity of her situation.

Why? Again Dorothea's conscientious question to herself in *Middlemarch* about the real scope of her emotional entanglement is pertinent; "Was it her event only?"[8] In the case of the woman's wordless sexual encounter, it is not only her event—emotionally. From another aspect, it is only her event, physiologically, in its consequences for her. In just this lies its simplicity. The reason I'm describing (apparently so conservatively and complacently) the minor violence of disrupting an assumption of untrammeled romance as falling to the woman's lot isn't only that, much as we might wish it otherwise, this sexual division of linguistic labor remains the way of the world. It's also that it's her reminder of her physical vulnerability which must point the man to his own biology as something independent of him, with its own repercussions; it's a way of turning him into a thing, even if maybe a flatteringly potent thing. The amorous moment is redescribed matter-of-factly, the instrumentality of his part suddenly exposed. The man could perfectly well ask the question about contraception himself. Of course. Few do.[9] Yet perhaps it's easier to say to a woman, "Could you get pregnant?" than for her to say, "You might do this to me," because the instrumentality is done away with and causes no intrusion as soon as it's assumed, taken on, by its owner. (This comment enacts a positively archaic view of the passive female part and the active male part in fertilization, but whatever its vices and virtues, this remains the prevalent understanding of the relation—and for very sound reasons.)

If shyness grips both parties or if the man doesn't mention the matter because he supposes she's taken care of it, or because by that stage he doesn't give a damn, then, unlike Lear's warning to his youngest daughter that nothing will come of nothing, something can certainly come of (saying) nothing. Conception can be consequent on many varieties of linguistic inhibition: a woman is slowed, not by her sexual but her verbal hesitancy, only to realize that before she's got the cautionary words out, the deed is done. Then there's indeed a pregnant silence. . . . But surely this is a terribly disappointing and banal version of philosophy in the bedroom; what's the point of scrutinizing this very ordinary dread of breaking across a discursive context? Only that it may show that the one affected by linguistic inhibition isn't in fact prudish or coy about particular words, but rather is seized by a habitual tendency (however misplaced in this instance) to shield everyone, herself included, from disrupting the whole context of verbal expectation by her utterance. Perhaps in some still unmelted corner of her brain she was silently, ferociously calculating the abstruse arithmetic of her so-called safe period, while the event overtakes her. Her failure to make timely use of a means of contraception which requires mentioning it on the spot is, then, a more elaborate question than the charge against her of simple fecklessness or recklessness admits. For the whole business of *mention* is no light thing.

This observation, though, isn't at all to recommend linguistic inhibition. It's only to remark that something generally useful—an alertness to verbal context—can, on occasion, be disabling. To someone who's alone, linguistic disinhibition comes more easily: the reason people curse blindingly if they trip on the pavement while they're on their own, but not if they're in company, is not their dishonest gentility, but their lifelong training in linguistic accommodation to others. And, as for the argument that if you do it you should be able to talk about it, we all know there's no necessary link between engaging in liberated behavior and engaging in uninhibited talking. There may even be a negative relation here. If we're to use this highly questionable term *inhibition* at all, then its commoner implication of sexual inhibition is doubtless far more readily overcome than is verbal inhibition. This exchange offers, among other things, a fine satire on this fact (while neatly rebounding on Gore Vidal's hapless interviewer, who had *not* hesitated to inquire):

Interviewer: Your first sexual experience—was it with a man or a woman?
Gore Vidal: I was too polite to ask.[10]

Or am I wrong to extend my comments, reliant as they are on these generalities about linguistic accommodation, to the particular scenario of the conception which is consequent on wordlessness? For isn't this example really a consequence of emotional inhibition rather than of linguistic inhibition? Surely such evasive vagueness shows immaturity, such cloudy and tremulous romanticism is plain silly in its dated refinement of silence, and it shows a risibly adolescent refusal to face the world. As if feminism had never existed! To be adequately heterosexual must include taking responsibility for its practicalities.—It's just this kind of brisk judgment that makes me want to demur, though. For there's an anxiety, far more complicated than teenage ineptness, about transferring words, which are fine if spoken in one place, into another place where they could be heavy-handedly disruptive, as if they'd failed to understand the occasion of their own being and were out to sabotage it. This general hesitancy then extends itself, however ill-advisedly, to the particular case in the bedroom.

An automatic decorum (for decorum is not at all at odds with passion) will try intuitively to maintain a balance. Bathos loses this. The lapse of bathos lies in the taxonomies of rhetoric; a sudden ludicrous lowering, at which embarrassment surges forward, a swift descent from the elevated to the mechanical, and a resulting deflation of mood. For the act of redescription implicit in our scenario is easily tipped towards the bathetic: so here is not, after all, a union of desiring passion but actually a threatened union of sperm and ovum, indifferent to the egg owner's romantic thoughts. Both of these descriptions, the biological and the emotional, will hold good in action, simultaneously; but they are usually fused in themselves, without requiring comment. It's the question about contraception which necessarily, rightly, and forcibly tears them apart, and by addressing it, isolates the one aspect, the bodily. We were trained as children not to point, and especially not at other peoples' physical features or peculiarities. But the question does point. As it must, it points unflinchingly at the presence and the potential of semen.

Timing is all, in comedy as in ejaculation. The woman who, overwhelmed by the occasion, does not speak in time is unable to make more than an ambiguous or ineffective interruption in her misconceived effort to preserve the occasion's integrity. Yet all this elaboration of verbal inhibition, this hesitating so as not to disrupt an assumed mood—this results in what's lamely termed "an accident" (also the euphemism for what befalls the small child too embarrassed to ask to go to the loo in time). The other standard euphemism, "I just got carried away," actually describes someone who was carried into the iron grip of linguistic inhibition.

The selective unmentionability of body parts is sheerly contextual; a naming of parts in the doctor's surgery is very different from the naming advocated by the advice manuals' heart-sinking insistence on clear communication and on directly conveying preferences, "telling what you want and where you want to be touched." Language becomes grotesquely pornographic when it's inept to its occasion, in a chilling *can-you-feel-anything-when-I-do-this* effect. Likewise, the instance of the woman not quick enough to speak out demonstrates the difficulty of verbal context, rather than of verbal content. It takes boldness to disintegrate what is (or what she takes to be) the high emotion of the moment by saying "Wait!" and inducing a response from her partner in a different register from the supposedly obtaining one. Here's the stuff of black comedy. The context may be believed, indeed experienced by the sufferer from linguistic inhibition to be one of profound romance, of making love. Whereas her companion might not labor under the least illusion that any love is being made at all, and might be deterred by her reminder only because of the mild nuisance of the interruption.

While public linguistic ritual exists to make the authority of its context evident to all, we're primed to believe in the liberty by contrast of private emotional exchanges. But these, too, are deeply rule bound. Their rules are harder to acquire, and all the harsher for being unwritten. Because they hold sway in private, unchecked, they're congenitally prone to misreadings, both comical and grave. The silence which had tried so conscientiously not to shatter a context may end up by shattering more than one life. Or with luck you might end up with a very nice baby which owes its existence to the triumph of linguistic hesitancy over good sense.

Not, of course, that verbal delicacy always falls on the side of delicacy of feeling, hesitancy before the prospect of harming another's feeling—not that delicacy can't coexist with violence. Killing can be mentioned with exquisite refinement. Or with the appeal to the tactfulness of a silence which has perfectly understood the murderously unspoken as that which is, after all, better left unsaid.[11] Then many linguistic contexts cry out to be ripped apart. Social and political upheavals always entail the end of accommodation in favor of verbal attack, linguistic disintegration, vehement terminological overthrow. Change hears and speaks the jarring, the tactless, the iconoclastic, and at its height it will bring thing-being unashamedly back into words.[12] Sometimes what's politically demanded is not linguistic accommodation but linguistic dislocation. This takes practice, the labor of the counterintuitive. For some, if few, purposes, one might have to grow a tongue thick as a thick skin.

There is, though, one happier alternative for the sexual vignette. Again it demands speaking out, but of a very different kind; for the protagonists, who unexpectedly realize themselves to have been caught in the resounding clash of passion and biology, to acknowledge and voice its comedy to each other. The one-sided experience of this situation would read it, disappointedly, only as bathos. For the saving grace of humor, it always—as they say about the act of conception—takes two.

SIX

"Lying" When You Aren't

*

Nothing, on occasion, can make you feel so guilty as telling the truth.

Here I don't mean that old and time-honored business of deliberately conveying a lie through the flawless contrivance of speaking the literal truth. Nor do I mean the truthful alibi, where the alibi is a self-conscious assertion of innocence which happens to be factually true but which masks the real emotional dimension; its literal truth is belied by its situational untruth. What I have in mind, rather, is that feeling of emitting an aura of lying, and the corresponding fear of not being believed. Where actually you aren't lying at all, you sense yourself caught out in some culpably artless lie. Rationally you ought not to have this impression of your own exposure; so you open yourself to your own reproaches at entertaining such disproportionate sentiments, and often in some trivial circumstance. For, perversely, it's worst with someone you don't know well, an acquaintance or even a complete stranger. This feeling of lying although you're telling the truth is something you'd expect to arise in a hotly charged drama, where all is ripe for contorted guilt to rear up. Yet its sharpest occurrences seem to stem from the most ordinary of everyday excuses, such as turning down some social invitation or accounting for some accidental minor lapse on your own part. Then why ever should you be clouded with a bad conscience here, when you know that what you're offering by way of explanation is perfectly true?

Or is there even any real question to be raised here, for isn't this an obvious case of plain guilt at work—the unease of the suppressed truth, as encapsulated in Cocteau's "I am a lie who always speaks the truth"[1]?

A few common examples, first.

Imagine someone who, on the evening of a party which she had long planned to attend, gradually realizes with a sinking heart that, despite all her earlier and serious intentions of going, she really can't make it. She has a severe cold, her head throbs. The only thing to do is to telephone now, at once, before the party gets going, and make her excuse which is, after all, absolutely true. At once the trouble sets in. She pauses before she gets to the phone. Certainly she does not want to gain—or worse, put the seal on—a reputation for rarely turning up, for being standoff-ish, morose, sunk in her solitude. Anyway, she tells herself, people are always somehow interesting, she likes them, doesn't she, and aren't these social events always gloriously unpredictable, for someone might drop some remark enigmatic enough to keep her happy for weeks. But not only does she feel dreadful, she has no energy to glamorize herself for the occasion, and anyway these days the long labor of beautifying her-self bears little fruit. She has no car at the moment. Keen though she is for women to reclaim the streets and the freedom to walk alone at night, she also realizes that some streets of the inner city have already been re-claimed by those eager to relieve the said women of their handbags and bank card numbers. Is this, she wonders, the real reason for her hesi-tation, a conservative new nervousness she'd rather not acknowledge? Then why not find a taxi? Is it some secret meanness in her which makes her hesitate? And why, she wonders, should she be feeling such anxiety? Realism tells her she'll hardly devastate her hosts by her absence. It will probably be a large party, she's not their intimate friend, and anyway, she reflects ruefully, her presence could by no means be reckoned to bestow any especial glitter on the event, or to cast an aura of vivacious wit. A few seconds after her call of excuse, they'll have gone back to uncork-ing the wine and setting out the smoked salmon, retaining no trace of her in their suitably preoccupied heads. They'll be satisfied by her recital of socially expected manners; they're really not going to be interested in whether or not it also happens to be true. Or is that she has no confi-dence that she'll find anyone to talk to there? Repartee with strangers is not her forte, and anyway everyone knows that at parties no one can ever really talk to anyone else, and then anyway everyone else will be there in couples, and anyway these days she's scarcely likely to be picked up by anyone, and anyway coming home alone will deprive her of the only real pleasure to be had from such occasions, the pleasure of holding a post-mortem on the event with your companion—and anyway, can she really have become this reduced, this childish? Abruptly she makes her telephone call. She does feel terrible, but she also tries to stuff all the severity of her cold into her voice, she coughs theatrically, ringing so hollow in her own ears that she's sure her hosts are hearing her true excuse not only with suspicion, but with contempt for her amateurish acting skills. She protests too much and realizes it, but she has no way back to safer ground. The Player Queen, of whom Gertrude observed that the lady protests too much, was no innocent.[2] Our lady, though, is not only speaking the truth, but in her desperate attempt to make sure it's conveyed to its audience, realizes she's overegging it. Her white lie which was never one, but which felt to her, its speaker, as if it was, has rapidly darkened in its telling to the semblance of a black lie. Dispirited, she hangs up. Really she'd wanted to elaborate absurdly, to insist to her hosts, "But I'm not usually like this; anyone will tell you I'm terribly reliable." Only the sheer impossibility of adding for good measure "And I really *am* telling you the truth, you know" had stopped her.

The irony, she realizes now, is that any half-fluent lie would have sounded far more truthful than the truth. It would have been much easier for her to convey her essential truthfulness (to her own ears as well as to her hosts) by departing from her well-worn but honest excuse, and instead enact a projection by inventing a safely uncheckable story: "I'm so sorry I can't come, an old friend of mine, she's someone you've never met, has just turned up here out of the blue, she's in a terrible state, really distressed, I couldn't have put her off, I'll have to stay with her until she calms down a bit, which looks as if it'll take all night, of course if she does come round, I'll bring her along later if that's OK with you . . ."

Too late. And by now she feels physically even worse. She reminds herself of a child who didn't want to go to school and cried so hard that soon she managed to make herself truly ill. Yes, her situation really is infantile; and it's also the suffocating frustration of the child who's unjustly accused and who cannot make herself believed, who shrieks and weeps unstoppably until she's almost sick, or else collapses into a hysterical pseudoconfession to satisfy the parent's wrong accusation.

When the stalled partygoer realizes that somewhere in the course of her self-beratement, her bad cold really had intensified considerably, relief washes over her: just as she knew all along, she really was feeling far worse than just mildly unwell; she's now positively feverish, couldn't conceivably have gone out, all along she must have had a real viral infection, and now, look, over a hundred degrees, the thermometer confirms it. . . .

She is certainly overwrought. Then doesn't this ordinary vignette plainly testify to her buried guilt—guilt at her real wish not ever to go to the party? To her secretive, no, her unconscious, antagonism toward her official friends? After all, Freud's gallery of incompetents, his criminals from a sense of guilt, did wrong to try to assuage some a priori guilt, which arose from their unconscious fantasies of already-committed crimes.[3] And surely this woman wouldn't feel such overblown guilt if she wasn't burdened by her own unacknowledged hostility.

Let's suspend comment for a while longer, though. Here's another unexceptional occasion for the uttering of excuses: having a habitual handicap which debars you from participation. Someone has a chronic illness, let's say a virulent form of arthritis, and on some days, unpredictably, it will flare up so that he can't travel in to his office. Each time he rings in to explain that he can't make it but will have to work from home today, he feels more and more like a liar who's not only deceitful, but is committing the worse sin of boring those expected to believe him. While his claim of incapacity is utterly true, and he's entitled by arrangement with his boss to take these painful days off, he still fears the concealed derision of his colleagues. He imagines them thinking that his tedious unoriginality is an additional affront to them; could he not, if he so trades on their goodwill, at least be heard to be trying to make it convincing by injecting a little effort into his deceitful story—couldn't he go through the motions? He hears polite boredom in the secretary's voice as she takes his familiar but truthful message with no flicker of interest. He feels as unconvincing as if he were saying that his grandmother had died and he had to attend her funeral. Which reminds him, his one surviving grandmother, who's somehow tottered through to her nineties, has seemed especially fragile of late. He groans at the prospect of telling yet another truthful lie, by which he means another truth that will sound like a lie. So his only way out is to furnish some baroque embellishment in order to make the unvarnished truth appear truthful. He resolves bitterly that, come the day he really will attend her funeral, he'll instead claim to his colleagues that he's been unexpectedly summoned to preside over the marrow competition judging at his home village's horticultural show. Let them swallow that one!

Here's a third unexceptional instance of guilt-ridden truth telling. Its cause isn't laden with a charge enormous enough to explain its anxiety, and in this respect it resembles the disproportion panic of the party guest, and the nagging irritable unease of the arthritic. This time, it's the common plea from ignorance or incompetence: "But I didn't understand what I was supposed to do." On the Prague subway you could encounter an inflexible bureaucracy which made no concession to the bewildered foreigner. So an imaginary traveler knew she'd made careful efforts to buy the right ticket, yet had still managed (the instructions scant, only posted in full in Czech) to buy herself a child's ticket instead for one leg of her journey. The inspector pounced, glittering. Her explanations in weak German that hers was a genuine mistake cut no ice. Marched into his office and charged with deceiving the railways, she was threatened with the confiscation of her passport and with the arrival of the transport police. She suspected that this inspector knew perfectly well she'd made a genuine error, but perhaps he'd be rewarded, if only by his gratified sadism, for the day's tally of idiot tourists he'd netted. The more she pleaded, "But you can see yourself I made a mistake; look, these fares glued on the station wall are explained only in Czech, which I'm sorry I can't read. I'm hardly likely to cheat for the sake of saving some small change," the more the police were invoked. Indignant shame choked her. Reason told her this was merely a bureaucrat at his work, as if Central Europe was simply and zealously playing out its literary part. There was no need to take it personally, for she dimly recalled that Kafka's *The Trial* began, "Someone must have been spreading lies about Josef K., for without having done anything wrong, he was arrested one morning." Yet soon both sides, the ticket inspector and the tourist, were in the fierce grip of the official emotions allocated to their respective positions. Her insistence that she'd made a genuine slip and should not have her passport confiscated intensified, as did the inspector's glacial insistence that this was exactly what was going to happen.

So far, so banal: there's nothing recherché about working yourself up into a state of high feeling when you suspect that your unvarnished account of things won't be enough to carry the day. It's much as de Tocqueville wrote of party politicians; they were "often accused of acting without conviction; but my experience goes to show that this is much less frequent than is supposed. It is just that they have a faculty which is precious and indeed sometimes necessary in politics, of creating ephemeral convictions in accordance with the feelings and interests of the moment."[4] Still, our tourist's response to this skeletal scene of capture and threat, yet in which nothing personal to her was at stake and the matter was an ordinary blip in an ordinary transaction, was to feel a persisting intense guilt as if she were lying—and especially when a large fine was extracted from her. But why such passion in a routinely aggressive scenario of evident impersonality? Why should she have burned with vexation and mortification, since the incident had exemplified an official's indifference to her person, and to her veracity or her mendacity alike? Perhaps in his evident indifference to the truth of her excuse lies the whole key to her injured reaction. Then couldn't we simply conclude, not for the first time, that egotism is always the close companion of guilt?

Yet I persist in suspecting that there's a layer of language's peculiarity here which carries its own emotional charge and which, accordingly, is more precise a peculiarity than that of any generalized guilt. There's something distinctive in the intense discomfort of the truthful excuse, and this might be worth pinning down.

Surely, though, my fourth and final illustration below exemplifies the truth telling which generates guilt because of a strong wish to do the thing which has been repudiated? Here is where we'd *expect* the sensation of lying while telling the truth to be at its most fevered pitch. It's the old case of "OK, I gave him/her up, believe me." I'll adopt a soap operetta's scene: having made the compound mistake of falling for another and then confessing my adultery to my husband, I assure him that I'm no longer seeing my lover. This is absolutely true. After a prolonged anguished struggle with myself, I gave him up rather than further imperil my marriage. Really I'll never contact him again. I'll leave him alone to establish some new life for himself, although I dread the thought of his succeeding in this. Without surprise I see, though, that I am unpersuasive to my husband, who's eyeing me with his newfound expression of skeptical contempt as I insist on the truth, repeating to him with an indignation that rings shrill in my own ears, "You can believe me or not as you choose, how can I convince you, oh alright, I know you can never believe anything I ever say again, I destroyed your trust and that's all my fault, it's unforgivable of me, but anyway the fact is, irrespective of what you think, I really have stopped seeing him, for good." (Here I just manage to desist from elaborating "and that's taken me a great deal of effort and misery.") This is where the lure of the sentiment "I might as well be hanged for a sheep as a lamb" beckons; evidently my husband won't ever believe me again, so given his permanent suspicion, why shouldn't I revert to seeing my lover in secret, since the emotional wreckage at home can't be salvaged and I'll always be treated as untrustworthy, whatever from now on I do or don't?

In all its gloomily hideous banality, this "Alright, I've given him up for your sake" sounds as if it must constitute outstanding proof that the feeling of lying while truth telling is born from a wish: the guilty wish to really still be doing what you happen not to be doing. But my sensation of lying while I reiterate that truth of my broken-off affair is far weaker. I know very well that I'm not lying. I also know that I rather wish that I *were* lying. This realization, though, doesn't intensify my guilt. On the contrary, it produces an effect of outraged innocence in me. How dare he look at me so coolly, so quizzically? Any guilt in me is shunted sidelong by an avalanche of my vexation, my grief, and my silly righteousness. That I can also recognize this emotional scenario as novelettish, and highly unconvincing, doesn't dispel it.

Such marital guilt as remains here is certainly consciously felt. Then doesn't it follow that a truthful social excuse is suffered all the more acutely because it is riddled with its speaker's *unconscious* guilt? Again I'd want to elaborate: if so, this is the unconscious guilt of language—of the language of the excuse. There is a decisive linguistic-emotional compound at work in the formulaic excuse. This possesses the overarching structure of a lie, irrespective of whether or not it happens on occasion to be true. That is why the more unexciting and routinely social the lie, the worse you feel about the outcome of using such a tired excuse—and exactly when it is the truth. In a situation replete with anguish, costly melodrama, and grave repercussions (like that of the marriage scene which, predictable as it is, is well removed from the modest occasion of the party lie), it's easier, ironically, to utter the truth through deploying a formula yet without being wrecked by guilt. For the thicker the emotional admixture and its injection of righteous resentment, the less ready to hand is that sharp guilt which springs, apparently so perversely, from a wholly truthful excuse.

The Formula

It was the dominating presence of a linguistic formula which determined our party woman's anxiety before and after her call of apology. The truer the excuse she uttered, the more acute her own bad conscience. Conversely, the more purely lying her excuse, the less her guilt would have been, just as long as her lie was not formulaic but mildly inventive while plausible, like the fictional friend who'd unexpectedly turned up distraught on her doorstep. At first sight paradoxical, the puzzle of why lying would work better than truth telling here melts away if we see that what's at stake is the impossibility of truthfully inhabiting what's an accepted social lie.

The party guest's true excuse that she can't come because she's unwell is also the set recipe for its occasion. It's prepared ready for use, and its easy availability makes it appear that its user must be lying. The form of the lie overwhelms. The truth teller's mortification is sharpened by her awareness that a whole convention of popular psychoanalytic thought becomes very knowing here, and gravely shakes its head to declare that there's often more truth in the lie, that her anxiety stems from her lie as the expression of her real wish. But this restrictedly psychological interpretation has overlooked the decisive and peculiar rhetoricity of the social excuse. This recalls Bertrand Russell's anecdote about G. E. Moore; "I have never but once succeeded in making him tell a lie and that was by a subterfuge. 'Moore,' I said, 'Do you *always* tell the truth?' 'No,' he replied. I believe this to be the only lie he ever told."[5] But this is, among other things, also a tale of the triumph of linguistic convention in entrapping Moore, that complacently worldly-wise convention according to which *everyone, as we all know, tells lies*. In the teeth of this, however flawless his actual veracity, he couldn't have agreed to it without sounding insufferably pious, or meretricious.

The mechanical air of the social excuse incites an automatic and indifferent skepticism in its hearers. Like any speaker the truth teller intuits this, and so she longs to insist on the truth beneath and despite the overarching verbal machinery. But the more she insists, the stronger her own sense that she's lying. Guilt persists oblivious to the real impersonality of the exchange, and to the insignificance of what's at stake. So the subjects of my illustrations (except for the deceived husband) understood that the unconcerned party hosts, the zealous ticket inspector, the boss's cynical secretary all, rightly, had no pressing personal interest in them. Structurally induced, their guilt was linked to the frustration of trying to truthfully inhabit a linguistic model or trope which is tacitly and collectively understood to be untruthful. This formula itself carries on its face its expectation of a white lie, so its latent darkness drains onto its speakers. It overrides them, whether or not they enter it honestly or mendaciously. "Conscience is the inner voice that warns us that someone may be looking," said H. L. Mencken, in a joke which refers supposed innerness to its actual externality; reciters of the perfectly true excuse fear that everyone may be looking at them because the formula itself is so shameless on the lips.[6]

I've given examples of poor truth tellers. But if you are a poor liar (in practice, the same thing) might that stem from your retained childish illusion that your real thoughts are legible to others, so that your halfhearted attempts at deceiving them always collapse? Isn't there a psychopathology of the truth teller? And doesn't compulsive truth telling mean you haven't grown up enough to abandon your illusion of being transparent to quasi-parental others?[7] But with the social lie, there's an extra complication of a rhetoric-induced anxiety, which is the shame of deploying the timeworn form precisely when its content is most true. It follows, as I've already hinted, that the better strategy for keeping a good conscience here would be, in fact, to lie—rather than to try to convey the truth through the shell of the standard formula. The woman who

couldn't make the party felt the impossibility of convincingly emphasizing to her hosts that she *really was* telling the truth. Such insistence
would have hammered away at the great structure of the social excuse,
but altogether in vain, and with an appearance of pettiness. Her effort
would have rebounded on her. For the genre of the social lie is always
tougher and more resilient than any contingently truthful speaker. The
formula exposes as irrelevant the honesty of its user. If our party dodger,
our chronically unwell employee, and our bewildered traveler are to be
described as neurotic, then theirs is a neurosis of a commonplace linguistic alertness to the trap mechanically laid for the importunate truth
teller by the existence of the social excuse.

In the face of all this, it pays to cultivate a determined naïveté instead. "It is more shameful to distrust one's friends than to be deceived
by them."[8] You might well extend this sentiment to anyone, if riskily.
So for allied reasons, I'll strenuously believe any student who tells me,
"I did write my essay but just as I'd finished it, my computer crashed
and I lost all my work." To retain my will to believe, I know very well
never to investigate the plausibility, technological or otherwise, of these
crashed computer claims. Stendhal recounts a classic tale of the need to
believe, especially where doing so entails exercising a wilful stupidity,
and where the heroine's insistence on this courtesy is quite right: "The
story of Mademoiselle de Sommery is well known in France; how, sur-
prised in *flagrante* by her lover, she boldly denied the whole thing. When
he pressed her, she cried, 'Oh! I see it all now. You don't love me any
more: you'd rather believe your eyes than what I tell you!' "[9]

Still, the social lie needn't be considered only as a terrible dominatrix.
Often it serves us. Today's equivalent of the housemaid primed to politely
rebuff callers with a "Madam is not at home" is the telephone answering
machine. It lies professionally on our behalf, whether or not we are in.
Unlike its owners, it is designed to lie without shame, and even when it is
fortuitously telling the truth because we really are out. At home, we wait
while it declares our inability to come to the phone, when the truth is that
nothing prevents us other than our tiredness or dread of an unwelcome
caller. The designers of such built-in messages achieved primly impene-
trable formulas; the tin lady who announces, "The person you are calling
is not available" covers a multitude of sins, as does a recorded "cannot

come to the phone right now." Not won't come, because languishing in the bath or frantically unblocking the dishwasher, but "unable" to come. We listen to our answering devices' prerecorded lies, and might blush as their plastic can't. Others are able to make a happy use of their own set messages: the young teenager's chirrup of "Love youoooo!" trills out at the end of each and every telephone call. Yet the automated affection of this prerecorded feeling is only a new flourish of old rules of politeness. Again it seems wrong to criticize, as visiting Europeans tend to do, the American cry in restaurants and shops of *Have a nice day!* on the grounds of its "insincerity." The formula as common currency may or may not be felt as hollow by its speakers, but to denounce the utterer is arrogant, and blind to the utterance's rhetorical life.

And many other linguistic formulas which lack any apparent content can be embraced happily. We don't habitually seek out and revere verbal authenticity or originality. Indeed the formulaic can get loved purely for its own sake, whatever its vacuousness. Imagine the Saint Valentine's Day card or bunch of roses which is despised by its recipient as a transparent example of commercialized sentiment and bad faith by calendar, yet is also longed for, eagerly expected. It is the thing that is wanted, but only insofar as it acts as a witness to her lover's willing subservience to this thing's sheer emptiness. This kind of recipient could even arrive at this recipe: he must really love me after all, since he'll go to the length of humiliating himself by acquiescing in this foolish commercialized custom, in itself so patently insincere; he's even prepared to go through the hollow rite of sending a Valentine card, anonymously of course, for my sake. He will be silly for me, according to the law not of the phallus but— if these are to be differentiated from it—of emptiness, self-cancellation, idiocy.

SEVEN

All Mouth and No Trousers:
Linguistic Embarrassments

*

Reflecting on the recently altered ways of talking in public about sexual behavior is a puzzling business, which threatens to turn melancholy. Is there a lowering of affect, not only in the new and brusque diction of sex but as evidenced by an easy violence of wider expression? Traveling, for instance, on the London underground on any weekend night, you'll hear groups of young women routinely calling each other bitches, "lezzies," and whores; and all this doesn't sound like well-meant banter, more a constant undertow of nervous aggression. This roughness of exchange isn't, then, restricted to an altered habit of talking about sexual behavior in particular. But I'm thinking more of the nature of the embarrassment which hits any speaker who hasn't settled into the recent styles of speech. A verbal blush: a mounting tide of red seems to rise over your unspoken and half-formed sentences as you sense that you're on the verge of being dictated to, by new habits of speaking that make you highly uneasy. You're being induced to adopt them. You want to oblige so as not to seem awkward, yet you can't: for a form of speaking is a form of feeling, and the feeling doesn't ring true.

What I have in mind is the invited use of a dully reduced language of sexual behavior, where this "invitation" stems from its ubiquity.

Is embarrassment produced in its reluctant speakers simply by what strikes them as an increasingly infantilized way of talking but which they aren't sure how to avoid, let alone criticize? Or is there some more intricate overlap between the broad linguistic embarrassment at *feeling ma-*

neuvered into a form of words, and this particular subject matter of sexual activity?

Even in raising these speculations one seems to be occupying the most conservative ground, all too well trodden. The apprehension runs down the decades that a coarsening of sensibilities is detectable in a silly public language of sex. In the last century and this one, more and more enfeeblement has seemed to obtain. What sounded obscene to the ears of one generation (a speaking generation is swift, can be measured to last a few months, or a few years) becomes the norm for the next. So *fucking* has achieved an air of virtually neutral description today—all depending, naturally, on where you stand as a speaker and listener—in contrast both to its previous standing as obscene, and also to the idiocy of newer euphemisms such as *bonking* and *shagging*. These are a nursery vocabulary, as if made up for the children by the grown-ups determined that they shall have harmless fun. That painful-sounding verb *screwing*, redolent of some less than lyrical action of metal on wood, has long since slipped from common use and has been replaced by *shagging*, which has an uneven lineage deriving, depending on where you pin your etymological faith, from the sixteenth century. For there's a solemn philology fond of retracing modern obscenities to their originally venerable and stouthearted peasant roots: this line we won't pursue. Meanwhile the newish and unpleasant expression "to have sex" aims to occupy the descriptive but still acceptable ground. It's utilitarian enough, and has certainly triumphed in its recent spread. But it's grossly inadequate, in that it suggests a kind of casual feeding.

One could run on. But whatever the examples, there's no way of talking that isn't highly charged; and adopting one verbal fashion indicates only that you've signed up for a trial membership of a discursive club. Maybe it's a kind of youth club, or else an old fogies' group. Or a self-help therapy group of the formerly sexually wounded. Whatever the reasons for an adoption of a speaking style, the selection of even the most outspoken remains no more, or less, than a social alignment. And to talk of selecting is putting it far too voluntaristically. Still, the emotional implications of the adopted mode aren't so straightforward. The constant use, for instance, of a puerile language of *bonking* needn't indicate its speakers' emancipation into a desirable lightheartedness or a down-to-earth frankness about sex. It might instead imply its devotees' deep immersion in their own embarrassment. The more vaunted the "frank speaking," the greater the speaker's real unease. The wide use of *bonking* could indicate not relaxed ease but its opposite; an unease so great and, of course, so thoroughly inadmissible that it has to shelter in its own creepy version of the nursery.

Or is this speculation that "uninhibited" baby talk masks its users' discomfort in itself a clutching at solace? For it could be comforting to suppose there's a reversal at work, that what's ostensibly open is actually closed — as evidenced by that would-be scandalous sexual entertainment television which secretes its unspoken etiquette, shown by its studio audience's loud disgust at any breach. Curiously old-fashioned in their self-conscious "outrageousness," such presentations take sexual behavior to be a kind of table manners.

Dismayingly, there seems to be something particularly and depressively British about the blend of prurience with babyishness, reinforced by much telejournalese. A wild hope to tame what's feared may underlie this widespread resorting to a cozy talk of sexual behavior. Yet such remarks as these I've just made are transparent attempts at consolation for the foreignness of a new culture, while the awkwardness of speaking into all this remains. Evaluate it as critically as we may, in practice we're great pragmatists, always quietly, rapidly assessing our audience as we open our mouths. The desire is powerful for accommodation to their likely talk. In the presence of someone new to me and when I can't fend off some discussion of sex, there's always a half-conscious calculation: is this someone who'll be thrown by the word *fucking*, which after all has such a graphic viscosity? Or is she instead someone who might feel that the phrase *making love* is too honeyed, even hypocritical, euphemistic? Or again, is she someone who might look for the false (or worse, the real) matiness of *bonking*? There is always the default position, which is to speak of *having sex*: but *having sex* is, with all its dullness, also an obnoxious and joyless expression. Yet in the course of a couple of decades at the most, it has rapidly conquered the middle ground. So perhaps my new acquaintance would feel more at home with the safe-sounding inaccuracy of *having sex*; inaccurate, because the reality is that we do not have sex, sex has us.

This sort of furious wordless hovering over the problem of how to talk is resolved as soon as the interlocutor responds, and clues are mutually snapped up. And in any event, everyone's susceptibility to being verbally embarrassed is enormously varied; you could indeed be quite free of it, and perfectly happy with the euphemism of the day. Or you could suppose there's no alternative, but anyway you aren't greatly bothered. For banal sex talk is certainly utilitarian—and to the point of being asexual in its effects. If it oils the chatter in the office or the gossip in the canteen, it's a social lubricant, rather than lubricious. So who minds it, then? Those who realize they're not part of that confident, or resigned, linguistic majority—perhaps they are older, living between changing regimes of speaking styles, or with a religious, a political, or an ideological sensibility which makes them wince. There are those who feel cornered by the wide use of, say, *shagging*, which condemns anyone who can't easily join in with it as puritanical, spoiling the linguistic party. Here a distinctive embarrassment on the part of those who underwent the process once known as sexual liberation appears; supposedly unshockable, and now bewildered by the prospect of seeming mealy-mouthed and prissy, you just don't possess a vocabulary with which to criticize a petty language of sexual behavior. The outcome is embarrassment at your own embarrassment. If it's the nature of embarrassment always to be further mortified by itself, here it forms a hall of mirrors. Here, too, antipornography feminism hasn't been incisive; the false association of feminism with an antiseptic attitude to sex has further dimmed much public thought. Nervous that to raise an eyebrow would condemn them to the suspicion of reaction, a generation of soi-disant radicals can't bear to think that, in monotonous obedience to the cycles of time, they've turned into today's radical conservatives. Alarmed by an apparent emotional-linguistic degradation which surrounds them, finding themselves entertaining unhappy thoughts about the silly representations of sex to which their children are exposed, at the same time they also fret that the forces of reaction must indeed have seized them. They fear to catch in themselves the sour tut-tutting of the once-eager old.

But maybe there's still help for them. As a first step, I'll propose a short defense of their embarrassment.

Any sheepishness at naming sexual activity in reductive terms is really an emotional-linguistic hybrid; hesitancy and stalling before such etio-lated diction isn't merely ideological. Pausing, mildly vexed with yourself for not just being able to join in, while you thrash silently around for an alternative, results from your will to give the linguistic formula the slip. You feel the might of the looming terminology, and it incites you to wrig-gling evasiveness. Yet another layer of embarrassment stems from your very efforts to steer clear of the formula, as if through them, your own labored prissiness were revealed. Or your mortification might equally lie in enunciating the set terms, but with inward misery. You obey, as you secretly demur. Aware that you'd stand out by not following down the designated speaking path, you speak camouflage. To inadvertently make yourself stick out in your own language is always wretched.

Some similar feeling marks a speaker's sense of some distinctive-ness or idiosyncrasy in her own pronunciation, once she notices it. A completely undeliberated and automatic accommodation to my listeners makes me lengthen my northern vowels in the direction of the southern speech I'm ringed by; not because of any private self-consciousness but because my speaking doesn't want to pull attention toward itself as a noise. For I know how distracted by any unfamiliar accent or mannerism of speech even the best listener is. Or I'll try hard to subdue my stammer from overwhelming what it is that I want to convey. That is, the desire to not be heard first and foremost *as a speaking thing* is characteristic of linguistic embarrassment in general. And this characteristic holds sway even where the content of the occasion of speaking is sexual.

To illustrate what I have in mind by the problem in hearing oneself as the sexually speaking thing, I'll name three artificially prized-apart sorts of linguistic embarrassment in the case of vacuous sex talk. But they are, in practice, fused; and both their interest and their intracta-bility lie in this very fusion. First, a specific *reification embarrassment*. By which I mean inescapable and, I think, a benign and useful embarrass-ment about uttering a language of reification (to take a chip off the old marxist vocabulary). Naturally, reification is a fine thing in its place. A conversation with a doctor gets easy enough once the threshold of nam-ing has been crossed; here there's no pretense to anything except clini-cal description, and an unambiguous context rightly triumphs over any initial awkwardness. Yet this first linguistic awkwardness is inescapable and unsurprising before it crosses into the new language of the medical setting. There's a distinctly grammatical or syntactical aspect to reification; the very word means making a thing out of what is not a thing. So the feeling of embarrassment at using an instrumental language of sex shouldn't be imagined as a failing of those who are repressed. It springs from trying to describe something by means of a verb, yet something not lived in such a way that it can be conveyed as behavior. The trouble, though, isn't only the enfeebled playground tones of today's common verbs of sexual activity. It's the necessary incongruity of the emergence of any such verb, whether it aims to be dignified or jocular, in public conversation. But no one need be embarrassed by embarrassment here. Not at all the same as prudishness, arguably it's a sound reaction to the eruption in the public sphere of what is private but grossly denatured in this translation.

Then, to repeat, linguistic embarrassment isn't to be despised. It's the emotion—I'd say, *the linguistic emotion*—that seeps forward when you find yourself shepherded in the direction of saying what you don't want to say. Rather than caving in to the idea that you must stifle your misgivings, it's more helpful in the face of such linguistic bossiness to properly register your own discomfort. There is sound sense in attending to your own nagging embarrassment. With linguistic embarrassment in general, you intuit that under the chivvying of standard talk, you're about to be forcibly revealed. With badly trivializing sex talk in particular, you feel that if you were to capitulate and talk the talk, you'd be not only exposed but wrongly exposed—not as what you truly are, but rather as what you aren't but are dutifully mimicking. It's far more shameful to be revealed as a *pretender* to petty obscenity than to be caught in the real thing.

Second, a further coating of historical embarrassment is laid over such ordinary reification-embarrassment; at least, this is a special embellishment kept for those in their late middle age. Yet why should you feel mortified by the very fact of your own embarrassment? Because another humiliation has arisen to interpose itself. This time, that historical shame of feeling that now you've become the curmudgeonly old thing who'd have tutted at your younger self in terms similar to those you catch yourself using now. Foolishly drained by overhearing your own conservative reactions to an increasingly vacant public language, you conclude that there's a generational unintelligibility. Yet you know that the idea of generational thought is itself a crude abstraction. In the same breath you recognize that yours is a worry of late middle age, if of an agitated middle age which hasn't yet managed to sedate itself. And you do not want to hear yourself reduced to uttering this: "Tsk! All this silly impoverished talk of bonking and shagging distorts the complex realities of sexual experience. It's just a new kind of alienation. In my day we certainly fucked around but at least we took it seriously, we had *sexual politics*, we had revolutionary ideals, damn it!"

Third, a broadly linguistic embarrassment lies in sensing the dictates of a weak terminology and then having to evade them by twisting one's speech around them. The uncomfortable sensation here is of being briskly led toward some grossly insufficient way of talking, because it's what's expected. — Expected who by? Not simply by whoever we're talking with, because they also swim in this transpersonal discursive anticipation. For there's a bullying linguistic expectation. It looks for compliance. Should we comply, we're subdued. Should we thwart it, our unease at doing so rises and intensifies.

And in the instance of how to pick our way through a world of speaking so heavily dominated by dire sex chat, all these three gradations of embarrassment overlap. The awkwardness of naming is embroiled with the awkwardness of demurring. A compounded verbal-emotional mortification appears in my secret hesitation in the face of some expected utterance I might have been able to use, were I not so hopelessly and culpably self-conscious. This embarrassment stops me on the verge of utterance to fish up a circumlocution, makes me quietly scan for a substitute for what I want *not to have to say*, or makes me reconfigure my syntax to suit the altered expression I'm now maneuvering toward, much in the way I'll try to dart in thought ahead of myself when, using a foreign language, I can sense towering over the end of my sentence the mood of a forgotten verb I won't possibly manage to retrieve in time. One quality shared by the embarrassments at joining in, or not joining in, some publicly coarsened reductive sex talk lies in the fact that we can hear its occasion approaching. We can feel embarrassed *avant la lettre*. This would be a curious sensation, if, as is often assumed, embarrassment really was only an effect of our unwanted exposure to other people.

It seems, though, that we can also feel a linguistic embarrassment in anticipation. Anticipation of exactly what, though? Where is the element of public exposure here: if embarrassment is usually to do with sensing yourself caught out in something shameful, then what, with your linguistic embarrassment, do you expose yourself *as*? As someone cajoled by the forcefulness of received diction into talking as a member of a linguistic constituency which isn't yours, into using infantile talk with which you don't concur, as if you were trying to curry acceptance with "the young," an illusion which also wrongs the actual young. Under the weight of such anticipated embarrassment, the standing of the word as thing solidifies, and the coming flavor of it becomes hard to hold in the mouth. A rough old injunction to a child dictated that a slip of her tongue would mean that her mouth would be washed out with soap. At least this backhanded tribute to the materiality of the word had the advantage of treating the power of utterance with a proper gravity. But after all, my embarrassment can always be sheltered by my silence; I can perfectly conceal it, and seamlessly utter a substitute. Then, given this option of silence, what is it about this phenomenon of embarrassment which implants its sneaky vexations?

It's an outcome, I think, of the prominence of language displayed as itself, and where all the words to say it differently appear, in the twists of the history of the present, to be compromised. But this is not an abstract of Language conceived as some immense and vague generality. Again, to isolate the distinctive effectivity of words isn't to set up and then make obeisance to some wily god of Language; that would be an unhappy move, since it would merely add to an overstuffed pantheon of capitalized deities. Rather it's just to observe the singular linguistic-emotional work of some phrase or a bit of syntax in the mouth or stuck in the throat; to register the exact and exacting pressure of some highly local demand of language exerting its delicate and peculiar force. Then on the other hand, there's always more to be said. And it will be, it will be.

EIGHT

"But Then I Wouldn't Be Here"

*

What kind of utterance is it that declares, I have the breath to make this noise only because *your* sort failed to stop me from ever drawing breath in the first place?

Such an assertion, springing from the very state of being alive, sounds irresistible when uttered in such a tone that to query it would mean wishing for its speaker's death. The clinching announcement by someone on an anti-abortion platform is that she herself would have been aborted (rather than adopted or fostered as she was) had a liberal law obtained at the period of her own conception. Her argument, issuing from the perverse privilege of a hypothetical almost-death, runs: "If abortion had been readily come by then, as you want it to remain now, then I would not have lived to challenge you today." In this vein, too, a speaker defending the rights of the disabled might point out that had prenatal diagnostic screening existed when her own mother was pregnant, she would never have been able to bear witness as a survivor of spina bifida. That's a different line of argument from reporting that the experience of living with a particular disability is far less debilitating than it looks from the outside, and concluding that economic considerations, justified by claims about the sufferings of the disabled, shouldn't dictate abortion policy. Instead, those declarations founded on the sheer condition of being alive run, "The law you propose in the name of choice, but which is effectively eugenics, would have seen to it that I was destroyed after conception. Disagree with me, and you want me dead. Or at least you want to erase me in retrospect; you want me never to have lived." To which the usual response from those seated elsewhere on the platform is a politely murmured, "I'm sure we're all very grateful that you are here with us today!" For the charge "You lot really want me dead!" is more of a discharge from a verbal blunderbuss which knocks out its opponent—unless she is icy enough to reply, "Quite right, I do." Yet who would walk, eyes wide open, into this set trap and then retort to the trapper's astonished injured face, "Actually yes, you'd have been aborted under any decently liberal law, had your mother so decided; and so what?" Knowing the implausibility of this exchange, the formulaic "I'd not be here now if you'd had your way!" rests on its power to stifle any such a reply couched in terms of unkindness which rebuffs the violence of the original unanswerability with more of the same. Such linguistic domination, though, will exert its own strains on itself, and despite its public effectiveness. Unassailable speech must be always readying itself against the permanent threat of approaching assailants. Its rhetoric is also a make of character armor, which does have its advantages; except that to go around clanking in a burnished carapace is terribly hot and burdensome for the armored ones.

There's humor in the not quite dead. Out of a satirical weekly, Freud clipped a joke about the old adage: " 'Never to be born would be the best thing for mortal men.'—But, adds the philosophical comment in *Fliegende Blätter*, this happens to scarcely one person in a hundred thousand."[1] The witticism aims straight at the heart of any fantasied not-being. But it would surely wither under the stern rejoinder of the one imagining herself in retrospect as the never-born, the eliminated victim of social eugenics. Here a decorum of *who* speaks stifles any comment on the mode or style of what's said. If there is a moral authority of suffering, as often asserted, this can readily become an authoritarianism of suffering. Fiercely imperative, it knows: *we* have endured, so *you* will listen to us. It holds out the gravitas of speaking out of a lived position: the bodily situated demonstration whose power is its very standing as utterance on the lips of the ontologically qualified utterer. This conviction of entitlement to authoritative speaking is underscored by a strong sense of propriety. Rightful speech, it's implied or stated, dwells in the mouths of the afflicted only. And this dictates the admissibility of what's articulated. So, as many hold today about the word *nigger*, it's permissible to use it only if you are it.[2] Others, though, are adamant that no black speaker should ever say it; the word is too historically disgraced, too demeaning, too grotesquely racist to sully any mouth, however teasingly companionable the user's intent. But in this instance there's at least an animated public debate; whereas in the case of abortion legislation, the asserted moral authority emerging from the "experience" of nearly being not alive rests on an unchallenged propriety which dampens dissent. The forceful appeal it makes from its supposedly fragile anchorage in this world can obscure any disagreement by others in the same boat. It allows scant room for similarly placed speakers to moderate that ringing "speaking as a . . . , I know," especially when the ". . ." represents a near abortion which was converted into the pure triumph of being.[3] A modern decorum of utterance rules, in a delicate marriage of linguistic terrorism and etiquette. And by implication everyone who was more or less satisfactorily adopted must, just by virtue of their early history, share this common and illiberal opinion; yet evidently they do not. Nor do you hear it said by people miserably brought up in a children's home. Yet "But I wouldn't be here now" is so arm-twisting a formulaic utterance that it subdues other private circumstances and conclusions. Were these heard, there'd be a permanent skirmish between contradictory stances, each based on differing personal experiences. For example, equally pitched at the claim from experience is that objection which tries to shake open the dominant form: "Well, I'm adopted too, but that doesn't mean that I'm anti-abortion, or that I wanted my mother to have lived under such a restricted law that she had to go through the misery of having me in secret, handing me over to a children's home then going on with her life as if nothing had happened." And, whatever the vexations of having to issue such a testimonial, it's only this kind of counterwitnessing from the ambivalent viewpoint of the insider which can crack the monolith of the deduction that all those who were once theoretically at risk of being aborted must axiomatically be opposed to a liberal abortion law.

But it's a hard task. By invoking the threatened extinction of their very lives, the negative privilege of the spokespersons for the near-aborted claims an unanswerability. These speakers' statements of their own retrospective vulnerability seems itself to be invulnerable. Yet from the standpoint of where it leads the argument, it isn't. The trajectory of this appeal to the condition of being alive isn't infallibly conservative, for

"But they wouldn't be here today if you lot had had your way!" is also occasionally proclaimed from the side of liberalism. Here "they" refers instead to those existing children who were only born thanks to in vitro fertilization technology, while the "you lot" refers to those opposed to the process because it entails discarding some embryos along the way. Or if one were to deploy the same logic as that of someone objecting that she herself would have been aborted under any liberal law, there's an obvious reply: "But then you wouldn't ever have been conscious to realize the fact of your own early destruction." This, though, is far too cool an observation for that smoldering terrain of feeling where the *you lot want me dead* is pitched.

It's here that today's liberalism runs into difficulties. For the recording and listing of hurt have long been prominent in the linguistic armory of bitterly recalled experiences: of the concentration camps, of diaspora, of poverty, of racist violence, of sexual hatred. And described experience has undeniably formed an effective polemic for many liberation movements, including feminism. So it's especially disconcerting for that strain of feminism which has itself drawn on the impassioned gravity of the "I feel" to have to register an equally ardent "I feel" from among the anti-abortion adopted, women and men determined to record their feelings of relief at being alive at all. For now the limits of the appeal to personal sensibilities as a ground for a liberal politics are suddenly and acutely in sight.

It is at the sharpest and thinnest point of the evidence drawn from the witnessing self—the point of this self's imagined near-vanishing from life at the abortionist's hands—that a listener can start to wonder whether too great a claim of entitlement consequent on the personal has been fed in. "But then I wouldn't have lived" becomes a variant of that excessively personalized strain of questioning, the *why me* genre, such as "Why do I have this incurable illness?" Or, to take a narrower example, the differently exaggerated personalizing of those badges and T-shirts which used to confront all eyes with "How Dare You Assume I'm Heterosexual." This slogan's drawback, formidable as a provocation as it was, was its attribution to others of their constant calculation about and keenly interested judging of its utterer's sexual disposition. But to glimpse such badges incited privately indignant or anxious rebuttals of

"I *didn't* assume. . . ." Were you forcibly hailed by this question on the lapel of the person sitting opposite you, one silent reaction was "But why should you so crossly assume that I'm the proper target of your sense of offense, that I'm remotely concerned with you and your sexuality, or that everyone, whatever their own sexual inclination, is busily assessing you—and then, worse, why should you dare, as you say, to assume that I'm heterosexual myself, anyway?" Another possible response to the brandished "How Dare You Assume I'm Heterosexual" was simply pragmatic: "I assume it, only because statistically it's a reasonable assumption; and this doesn't imply any antagonism on my part toward homosexuality." Whereas the decidedly antierotic nagging of the slogan itself was no advertisement for queer joy. Still, all onlookers realized that the badges' point was to make explicit a broad social presumption in favor of heterosexuality, rather than to take focused aim at any individual opponent. Nevertheless, the very syntax of "How Dare You Assume" did point its finger, if indiscriminately, at each and any onlooker. So this pseudo-personal accusation couldn't do otherwise than incite a myriad of efforts at personal exculpation. The ironic upshot was that its reliance on fingering individuals fetched up, not in rendering the personal political, but instead in provoking clusters of always personal but hidden rejoinders. In this manner the sought-for critical erosion of the public-private distinction instead ends up with a carping and secretive defensiveness.

To return, though, to the case at hand: as I said, it's often taken as read that, having escaped elimination yourself, your escapee status entails that you must vigorously denounce abortion. It doesn't. Nor does it mean that you must be deemed "self-hating" if you campaign for abortion rights. (Here, having just complained about the I tyranny, I am resorting to it, although in the minor key of *not-I*.) In a reworking of Kantian altruism, Wendy Brown proposes an idea of enlarging what one was born toward what one hopes for others: "I want this for us."[4] This stance requires imaginative unselfishness; where that's lacking, then far too much of the personal, understood as gain, is fed into the argument. But "I want this for us" could mean not "I want all the potentially aborted ones, as I'd have been, to be preserved by means of a more restrictive abortion law" but instead "I want other women to have the same freedom of choice under the law as I now have. And I don't want my own existence to be used to reinforce a claim which would burden existing lives." For I'm not compelled to make a universal stance out of just one aspect of my own history, the accident of my unwanted conception, magnifying it until it overwhelms all other considerations.

Yet "so you wish me dead!" does rest on an excess of self-reference, perhaps born of horror at the realization that you'd have been discarded as grossly substandard, had the technology existed to run a quality control on you before your delivery. Still, everyone's grip on life is, in some way, tenuous. Admittedly this common sense of our frail adherence to the surface of this world carries a very different resonance from that of specifically being a candidate for abortion due to disability screening as a national policy. But to pursue, for the moment, just the broader uncertainties: few people can be sure of having been unambivalently wanted by even one of their parents, while many realize or have good reason to suspect that they weren't. Yet surely such initial "wantedness" is overblown as a requirement for leading a life. That slogan of "every child a wanted child," which once rang out on proabortion marches, is as pious a eugenic sentiment as ever crossed the lips of a well-meaning but sheltered feminism. Not because of the burden of being terribly wanted and its cloying expectations—but because your subsequent life is not exhaustively determined by your initial desirability in the eyes of your progenitors. No doubt the conviction of having been wanted must be reassuring, especially in a modern setting thick with faith in the virtues (which lie so close to the old vanities) of self-esteem. But it's a conviction hardly essential to living and its inescapable trains of fortune and accident. You can be perfectly aware that to your mother your conception came as a sickening blow, that your father angrily denied paternity and left for good, that inept amateur attempts to abort you were tried: still, you find yourself stoutly in the here and now. And despite that private history of yours, you can still regret that abortion had been so hard to get in the past, even though its earlier availability would have guaranteed your own extirpation. You don't have to let a phantasm of your own infancy dictate your espoused cause; instead you can prefer to preserve the present relatively liberal law. Not, though, because of your own deathwish, although some will be quick to swear to you that this is the real reason lying below your apparent liberalism. But because you can, coherently, want advantages for others that you personally would not have profited from, or indeed would have died under.

The murderousness summoned up in my imagination by a reiterated "Had easier abortion choices existed in those days, then I wouldn't have lived" is really presupposing a choice made by my actual parent when faced with the charming reality of me—as distinct from the plainer scenario of an impersonal decision made by my potential parent to abort. This retrospective dread of the killer mother could and does hit many. We might all, the officially wanted and the illegitimate unwanted alike, cry out on occasion to our parents that they'd rather we hadn't been born. This may be all too true. (Certainly it's likely to become true for the duration of the moment that the parent hears that irritatingly self-regarding plaint.) From the maternal standpoint, your child may well have been no sought-after conception, but an oversight, a lapse, or the outcome of a merely halfhearted gesture at contraception; the decision to continue with the pregnancy may have been hard won, a slow resignation after the event, while pleasure in the child's existence may come late, if at all; some may always view its being with an inwardly cold eye; then the once intensely wanted child may disappoint, if its mother's roseate imaginings are shattered by its presence. To such common hazards of frank unwelcomeness, or the ordinary ambiguities of wantedness, can be added the very long odds against one's managing to exist at all. An endless string of accidents has preceded anyone's birth—which I'll see if I envisage the contingency of, say, my great-great-grandmother's birth and her own lack of success subsequently in preventing the conception of my great-grandfather, and then I multiply that kind of chance a millionfold to cover my own arrival. The world rustles with spirit adherents who never made it, the lost prospective souls of miscarriages, the near misses of unfrozen deselected embryos, discarded hopes. True that no such reminders of the wholly arbitrary nature of any life at all would assuage the misery of someone haunted by the prospect of her own nonlife, deliberately sought. But then there's advantage in taking that historical fact of your unwantedness hard on the nose—yet not staggering backward bleeding heavily from the impact. It could even be bracing to hear someone answer your cry of "You lot want me dead by means of your dreadful liberal abortion law" with a "Too right!" For if you ought "by rights" not to have made it into this world at all, yet you did so by a hair's breadth, then it's all the more quietly exhilarating to find yourself, against the odds, solidly alive. Yet at the same time, your full enjoyment of your own narrow squeak of an achieved life will, arguably, include your wish for others' liberty to enjoy theirs. And this wish for others runs more ways than one; it does not dictate on which side you must fall in or whose liberty you must conjure. By no means must it automatically propel you to the defense of the imagined unborn.

The linguistic showstopper of "But under your liberal abortion law, I wouldn't have existed" falls like a lead weight upon any exchange. It could only be bumped back into life (ultimately this will be the animation of comedy) if someone also who is similarly ontologically challenged else raises the retort "Nor would I—and so?" The fact that your loyalties aren't, in fact, preassigned by the nature of your conception makes for a likely dash into infantile combat with others who will all too confidently speak for you. The old war of "We are!" versus "Well, I'm not!" starts up. Mutual sniping has its field day. The liberal dissenter who announces, "Just because I'm adopted myself doesn't mean I'm going to join in with this antiabortion line" can sound foot-stamping, naively egotistical in her renunciation. This is because she's been forced to throw her own intensely personal claim against the universalized personal claim of "Your prochoice law would have destroyed all possibility of our existence." Her seemingly idiosyncratic assertiveness in declaring that she, for one, wouldn't have wanted to live at the cost of the immiseration of her mother's generation is the only recourse she has, even while through it she ends up apparently willing her own destruction. Imagined orders of death clash here. To counter those who repudiate readily obtainable abortion on the grounds that the murder of their own unwanted kind would follow, she lays tacit claim instead to shelter other women, reluctantly pregnant, through her own noble suicide.

Yet her stance is also latently humorous. Not because of its altruistic impulse, shot through though it may be with self-aggrandizement. But because an argument intended to contest the claimed sovereignty of experience (of life) has ended up by asserting the preferability of having no experience at all: "Well, speaking for myself, I'd rather never have been born at such a cost to others. . . ." Once uttered, this stance deflates itself.

Straight toward comedy is where all aspects of the claim from being alive must logically and inexorably go. If the antiabortionist sobs, keeping one eye open to gauge the effect of her rhetoric, "But you'd have killed me!" then the proabortionist declares, "Let me have died for you!" There's a fine example in the script of *The Life of Brian* of an apparent act of self-abnegation, but which has actually been dictated by the relentless grammar of its surroundings.[5] It comes at a point in the movie when a crowd of followers are flocking after their putative messiah and savior in the reluctant shape of Brian, who's exasperated by their subservient zeal:

> *Brian*: Look, you've got it all wrong! You don't need to follow me! You don't need to follow anybody! You've got to think for yourselves! You're all individuals!
> *Crowd*: Yes, we're all individuals!
> *Brian*: You're all different!
> *Crowd*: Yes, we are all different!
> *Homogenous Man [in crowd]*: I'm not.

NINE

Your Name Which Isn't Yours

*

Paying tribute to the oscillating supremacy of a first name, Gertrude Stein mused, "People if you like to believe it can be made by their names. Call anybody Paul and they get to be a Paul call anybody Alice and they get to be an Alice perhaps yes perhaps no, there is something in that."[1]

What there is in that is a readily recognizable conviction: the name is strong magic. Its powers are great enough to have become enshrined in the language as literary cliché, which is a truly serious achievement. Contrary, though, to the best-known and most worn of these clichés, the whole heartless plunge tombward that is *Romeo and Juliet* demonstrates that the rose by any other name would not, in fact, smell half as sweet.

But that's an instance of a warring clan, bloodily sensitized to the family surname. The first name that I carry is ordinarily free of grave consequences for me. What's more, in a strong sense it has extremely little to do with me. Which is at first sight odd, because what's ostensibly more intimate a marker than my own name? Yet the real impersonality of the personal name is exerted here where the promise of intimacy has faltered, and where that shard of language which is a given name functions much like a travel ticket or a luggage label. It's another of the unflagging paradoxes of "identity" that what individuates you is a ready-made badge pinned onto you by someone or something else. My name is sheer "extimacy." And it's something that I pull inside me to make it mine, drawing it in from the outside. But of course that's a hopelessly skewed description, because as a child I hear it and must half-consciously assume it several years before I'm in any position to reflect on it, whether dispiritedly or complacently.

In theory the named person submits, more or less gracefully, to this impersonality of her name, tacitly consenting to behave as if it were the personal moniker that it is not. (A *moniker* is a word which vexes the compilers of etymological dictionaries, but most conclude that it was originally a nickname taken by a hobo, derived from the Shelta word *munik*, or name, or else from the old Irish.) The named one bows to the thin fiction that the name is herself, that she must be Monica, and so *Monica* becomes her. For even though the venerable ordinances which once governed ritual naming have long been dissipated, nevertheless a surviving *structure of the act of naming* means that you must take on your bestowed name like a fate; even if you'd fail Nietzsche's acid test of being willing to be called it all over again in your next reincarnation. But again, this notion of "taking on" your name drifts too close to supposing a deliberate choice to submit; and it also forgets that a name descends in infancy, a time when informed consent isn't on. Necessary and thoughtfully considered as it may be, giving a child its first name is a small violence. It was, naturally, God who called the stars by the names they were to have; and the mute infant bearer is no better placed to object than they, though the godlike parental tyranny of naming will play out its repercussions for the rest of that child's life. A name can be changed later on by its bearer, but it takes fervent toughness to insist on it, to face down the self-consciousness of announcing, I am no longer *Alcina*, from now on do please just call me *Rodelinde*. But what is this acute embarrassment? Shouldn't abandoning some imposed name to substitute something better that you've selected for yourself be a straightforward and fully justified act of self-assertion?

Yet—at least in those worlds, the majority, in which public ceremonies of renaming no longer exist—this self-assertion is thwarted, and its frustration is just one aspect of the unfreedom which attends naming and being named. To start with, the happy anarchy of parental free choice of what to call your baby doesn't do anything to soften the imposition of that calling and its brutal finality, once done. And that apparent anarchy will anyway turn out to be propelled by its own unrealized compulsions—compulsions which operate not within the spirit of the namers, but within the strange autonomy of the name. Once termed a "Christian" name as a marker of its inaccessibility to Jews, the first name has always in some way been corralled by the policers of faith. Yet even in the most determinedly secular of societies, the child's name is still not witness to the unfettered play of a parent's fancy; it turns out still to be considerably bound, although now bound not by clear tabulations but by obscurer limits. The name hovers at some midpoint between the tattoo and the state register: the formal identity displayed by a passport or a social security number can readily be stolen but then replaced by a fresh number because it doesn't inhere, it's not embedded in the flesh — hence the great strength of the tattoo, which is. And the business of naming isn't, as the namer might hope, about capturing the particular child, finding something with charm and distinction to suit, or as the publisher's blurb for *Baby Names for the New Century* proclaims, "You want a name that gives your baby a foundation for forging a unique identity, a name that expresses your hopes for the future. Here is the 21st century approach to finding a name for your baby that perfectly reflects your lifestyle, your interests, and your heritage."[2] But naming is more about recording an inscription in a line of descent, however loosely, almost inaudibly, this has come to be demarcated; as a practice, naming just isn't designed to convey a refined and sensitive individuation. For if children weren't named but were numbered in the order of the exact moment of their national birth, like cars cruising out of a factory, each fitted with its license plate, then (fatal overtones of the concentration camp apart) such numbers, because arithmetically unique yet replaceable, would afford better means of individuation than the human first name, so easily duplicated that in any small town within a span of a few years a whole crop of *Amy Browns* might shoot up; while on the Internet, phantasms of slipping into other identically named lives can flash enticingly into view.

A grave weight is imposed on any child named for the dead, whether the heavy burden of a lost sibling, or the milder legacy of the historical dead; and in Jewish practice, a child can only be named after a dead relative. But if my name was not chosen under the sway of its inheritance from someone else, then it exhibits a defining arbitrariness. Is it, then, analogous with my looks? I didn't ask for those, either. They ruthlessly fix how I'm understood, they run out in front of me so that whatever I may hope lurks in a "true me," despite my shell, would have to be patiently disinterred from the ruin of my appearance which precedes me, and which precedes me far more immediately than my name does. To any devotee of the greater truth of the external, this is a dispiriting observation. At least I can change my looks, or somewhat, can embroider my skin with tattoos, sport a new moustache, buy myself triumphantly globular breasts, wax away my currently unfashionable chest hair, pluck my eyebrows into a quizzical crescent, and generally wrestle my undoctored appearance to the ground before I raise it up revamped in my preferred image. And it's far *easier*, more socially manageable, to undertake these acts of vanity than it is to effect that other vanity of changing my given name. For my name is only formally my property. It stems from other people; they gave it to me, but their imperious gift has arrived with no receipt by which I can discreetly exchange it. The same is true of my looks; and yet I have more latitude, depending on my wealth, to change my appearance than to change my name: why?

Unfathomable Fashions

Any first name appears to possess a seasonal and mysteriously collective life of its own. Suppose that no etiquette of bestowing an ancestral name survives and that its choice is not tied to those sanctioned by religious custom; then a shift in vogue for particular names seems undetermined. It's evident that a first name pins you relentlessly into your place of emergence, by its class overtones, its clumsiness or its melody, its religiosity, its cultural timbre, its brief fashionability. And while, admittedly, sex-neutral names are to be found, the resulting lifetime of unexciting confusion is hardly to be wished even on a bearer devoted to blurring genders. Yet this clear power of the name to pinion its carriers in place is subject to its own wavering prominence, its fluctuations in modishness; and as one sociologist of naming has noted, it is risky to explain changes in popularity by external social determinants.[3] Why do first names go in waves? In Britain *Abigails* and *Sophies*, *Daniels*, *Matthews*, and *Emmas* have surged up only to sink away again in great tides, with mysterious crosscurrents and undertows of *Joshuas*, and eddies of *Eddies* (the study of naming always compels facetiousness). No incisive reason can be adduced for the ferocious mass advance in the last several years of *Chloe*, a decorative but hitherto obscure Greek name which is today's most popular girls' name and which is racing as unstoppably across the female population of Britain and Ireland as another pretty Greek term, *chlamydia*.[4] As well as such seasonally high watermarks, there seems to be a diachronic rule of taste by which the names of grandparents and great-grandparents become no longer old hat but freshly alluring, like the return of *Lily*, *Maud*, *Charlie*, *Ruby*, while *Bert* and *Alfred* wait patiently in the wings to pass from present fustiness to renewed desirability. Yet to *Cecil* all hope of resurrection seems forever lost.

These seasonal upswellings are hardly a matter of fashion, if by fashion you mean the deliberately selective adoption of what is around. The frank copying of first names from the movies or television does, of course, happen. But the parent's common experience is more often, reportedly, of choosing some mildly original name for your child, which later turns out, greatly to your surprise, to be common everywhere in its same age group. This accidental uniformity seems to have settled in as relentlessly and silently as a thick overnight fall of snow. And it settled—whether despite, or more probably due to—all the forethought you'd taken to perform your christening task with apt gravity. You had aimed for something which wouldn't cause any stir of contempt in the playground, you'd clamped down your own wilder impulses, stirring though they'd sounded, you'd consulted with your friends only to be secretly dismayed that so many suggested the ubiquitous neutral *Ben*, you'd tried to achieve euphony with the surname, you'd steered clear of accidentally claiming national affiliations that weren't yours, you'd genuflected before all sensibilities, and you'd scrupulously considered the father's absolute insistence on *Margaret*, before the scream of his departing tires had relieved you of further need to be democratic. You had fancied something with some light history, so *Viola* and *Felix* were both briefly entertained, only for you to dismiss them as inflated, especially when they'd be used with the surname of Scruggs. Even *Mercedes* had hurtled across the far horizon of possibilities, to race mercifully out of sight again. But after all this prolonged sifting until the relief of the final choice of the best possible name, years later it's brought home to you that everyone else's—doubtless similarly calculated—siftings have only ensured that the school playground is swarming with other small *Jacks* and *Ellies*. *The Times'* annual published list of favorites confirms it; your efforts at discreet originality tempered with manageability have resulted in your children's names coming in at numbers 5 or 11 down the list of front-runners for their year of birth.

It's as if there's a collective unconscious dictionary of first names. It falls open annually at a particular page, to beam its choice out to the heads of the population of new parents. This is a population divided, inevitably, into widely differing swathes of taste. And yet no discernible logic governs each swathe in its own selections. If there is a rough class division in names, these boundaries are arbitrary, not sacrosanct, and soon slackened. So within a few decades, *Victoria* has slipped off the throne and into a crop top. The "free" choice of first names on the part of the namers is, given this peculiar effect of mass dictation by the Unconscious of the Monikers, a far less unfettered affair altogether. The dictionary that Robert Louis Stevenson envisaged as a prophylactic against acts of poor naming already exists, although in a form remote from the prudent deliberation that he advocated:

> But, reader, the day will come, I hope, when a paternal government will stamp out, as seeds of national weakness, all depressing patronymics, and when godfathers and godmothers will soberly and earnestly debate the interest of the nameless one, and not rush blindfold to the christening. In these days there shall be written a "Godfather's Assistant," in shape of a dictionary of names, with their concomitant virtues and vices; and this book shall be scattered broadcast through the land, and shall be on the table of every one eligible for godfathership, until such a thing as a vicious or untoward appellation shall have ceased from off the face of the earth.[5]

The book has come to be; but not as Stevenson's corrective.

The First Name as Influence

If our parents christened us "freely," and if such freedom really meant "occurring under some tacit or dimly realized constraint," then we can be in no doubt that we ourselves live under the lash of the name. Our names are what we have to inhabit as constituting us, willy-nilly. A few are lucky enough to be able to roll their names pleasurably on the tongue. Most of us would really have liked something more euphonious, more graceful, more neutral, or more resonant—or, if we were especially unlucky, less mortifying. As to the embarrassment attending a certain name, to suppose that it's really the nature of the person we've experienced which governs our associations with the name is mistakenly, excessively, reasonable; for the pure name at its moment of arrival at the christening has its own aura. Recognizing this unstable autonomy of first names, many countries have laws to curb the wild parent by pruning back the fanciful or the miscegenating choice. So under new legislation in Finland in 1991, *Athena* is barred as outlandishly un-Finnish; on the other hand, in cruelly liberal England, a child can in law be, and on occasion actually is, named after every player in an entire football team. Bestowing a ludicrous name is one instance in which the adult who's committed this act of child abuse—which is what it is—cannot conceivably mount the abuser's limply corrupt defense of "But I thought it was what he wanted," or "She seemed to like it." Only if you were wise in selecting your parents will you confidently inhabit their selection of the names in which you've grown up. Still, with some luck, life may allow you to forget all about your own first name. You'll not need to brood over it; you'll not be pricked into contemplating its unhappy associations, or needled by the taunts that, if it stands out, it will draw. My name in this respect is less like a definition but more like the shape of my nose. Not because both name and nose are, if with difficulty, malleable; but because both soon fall away from the regard of those among whom we move. A maladroit and lumpish Grace may often heave a sigh over the irony of her name, but for her acquaintance her own larger presence will in practice always overwhelm the resonances of her name's meaning. For the vivid impact of the person in the flesh dissipates the prior associations we had with her name, which melt away as soon as we meet its bearer; and as we know her better the name becomes almost forgotten, irrelevant, a separable overlooked thing. Any first name that slips away to vanish in use, that turns into a translucent element, and doesn't ever stick out in advance of its bearer is good to have. The ideal name would resemble water.

The tendency toward fading prominence of the word as such is gripping. It waxes and wanes in the intensity of its presence, its wavering resonances. And it's this very thingness of the word which exerts a lively gravitational pull. But while the distinctive repetition of utterance *may* sometimes come to tame the impact of an outstanding word, it habitually does so with a first name, so that even the most exotic soon becomes less striking simply through its being used to call a particular known person. Its tie to his uniqueness will drain away its own peculiarities and eventually sink them, until we come to say about our good friend to someone else, *Alceste, Alceste*, yes, I suppose that is an unusual name, but these days that never crosses my mind; he *just is* Alceste to me. So the awkward conspicuousness of the name as felt by the named person can be merely a benign individuation in the ears of others. They may reflect that each *Suzy* is so very different from any other. To herself she is not different, and her first name can stick awkwardly, a foreign word pinned to her; whereas to those who call her by it, it eases away from view, quickly losing its distinctiveness through familiarity.

A first name is, in this respect, greatly unlike other kinds of words, on which repetition habitually acts oddly, even incalculably, on their original force (which is where both the power and the vulnerability of political diction lies). With the noun especially, reiteration can weaken or bleed it, can distort it, can ironize it; and it will also expose its sonorous or the graphic queerness, returning it to view as a thing. "Repetition is never an inert affair, despite its mechanical fidelity. Say it, read it, echo it often enough and at short enough intervals, and the word suffers a mutation, its thingness abruptly catapulted forward. It begins to look somewhat comical or grotesque in its isolation — and this folly soon seeps over the reader too, who may feel sheepish to be so greatly struck by the repeated thing-word. Is this strangeness only in the violent decomposition of the word, all meaning evacuated, into its typological clusters of characters in their graphic shapes? If one were to think, conventionally, of the word as animated solely by its meaning, then through the process of reiteration alone, one would be suddenly confronted by the word's corpse, or its waxwork. Whether by the enforced prominence of its sounds, or the odd look of the letters themselves, to see a word printed many times over on a page makes it start out, and this exposed arbitrariness is indeed queer.

This dizzied us as children. Sheer repetition exaggerates the sign into a wonder."[6]

First names, though so often repeated, escape this tendency. And one strong habit of considering what names do is far less concerned with their thingness, instead weighing up the possibilities that they are mere denotation against the risks of their covert influence. A trust in the transparency and neutrality of the given name marks a subsequently chewed-over passage in which John Stuart Mill, writing in 1843, held that the meaning of a name is simply its referent: "Proper names are not connotative: they denote the individuals who are called by them; but they do not indicate or imply any attributes as belonging to those individuals."[7] Mill's thoroughly rational briskness is far removed from the hoary tradition of the determining magic of given names. Here there's a strong vein of speculation much like Robert Louis Stevenson's: "In after life, although we fail to trace its working, that name which careless godfathers lightly applied to your unconscious infancy will have been moulding your character, and influencing with irresistible power the whole course of your earthly fortunes."[8] The habit of wishful naming has long flourished, and believers have always been sure that aptly chosen names might avert danger, ensure a long life, aid recovery from illness, and bestow admirable characteristics. Whether practiced by the Chippewa tribe or by the Puritan tribe, rightly directed naming would make a bearer led by a noble vision, or stouthearted in God. But this outcome naturally demanded the sanction of custom to make it work. The name that tries to retrieve the dignity of some already lost or dislocated genealogy can, despite its best aims, work as a handicap if it's used where its context of authority has been eroded. Recognizing this, the business journalist Tannette Johnson-Elie argues for giving African American children one "white" name too, so as not to sink their chances of being called to professional job interviews, given the real evidence of discrimination on the basis of applicants' first names: "The reality is that we live in a society where it helps to have a white-sounding name and where the colorful, Afro-centric names that many black parents choose may actually work against their children. . . . In other words, you're more employable if your name is Emily Walsh or Brendan Baker than if your name is Lakisha Washington or Jamal Jones." While acknowledging the legacy of imposed slave names reclaimed today as a spur to parents' inventiveness, she concludes pragmatically that if only African American names were to become common in corporate circles, then the business world would stop rejecting CVs bearing them—but meanwhile some sleight of hand is advisable: "It's OK to name your child, let's say, Dashiki. But here's a suggestion: Use a traditional first name such as Jason or Karen so that on a resumé he can become Jason D., and she can become Karen D., for example."[9] Since a dashiki is a style of collarless shirt, the complete OK-ness of Dashiki is debatable, but the writer's point remains: to be conspicuously Africanist of first name on your application form demonstrably keeps you off today's American corporate ladder—so, pass as white on paper, in order to get seen at all. To be named Dashiki signals that you have been inscribed in the communion of your kind, but that's not the kind that currently manages and patrols economic power. The argument is that given the brutal state of things, your advancement depends on contriving to be interviewed in the first place, if at the cost of strategically bleaching your first name enough to ensure your arrival in the flesh.

The Benign Impersonality of the Personal Name

If handicapped in a racist world by such well-meant ethnic naming, let alone vulnerable to being cursed by frivolous naming, you'd be in a far worse fix if you were to risk dying unchristened altogether, and so unreceived into any communion. For Catholicism, the baptism of innocents could enable their safe passage to the next world, as a timely formula saved the infant soul; so convent schools in the 1950s prudently taught a short ritual for baptism, just in case you came across an abandoned baby at the roadside, for if it died without the words being pronounced over it, its soul would languish in limbo. Such helplessness in the absence of the right utterance extends to adulthood. For while someone else endowed with the sheer power of the formula could baptize or rebaptize you, you can't normally do it for yourself; the whole essence of even renaming resembles baptism, in that the one renamed is passive under the dictation of the bestowed word's ceremonial authority.

You might think that the instance of adoption would offer an exception to this rule, in cases where a different name was attached to you to obliterate whatever you were called at birth. The authority to rename yourself could follow your rediscovery of your original name, if you greatly preferred what you eventually, as an adult, found on your birth certificate. But here again there's no letup. The harsh truth is that even your original name does not belong to you; it belongs to other people and always did, and that won't change now. The *Maureen* of twenty-five years' standing cannot really interest her friends in addressing her as the *Georgia* that her birth certificate declares her natural mother to have ambitiously deposited in her departing wake. It is easy enough, once armed with a deed poll, to change your name to the satisfaction of banks and passport offices (I write in a Britain which does not yet impose national identity cards). It's harder to persist in announcing to old acquaintances, "Sorry but I'm not *Maureen* any more." And hard, too, for the friends to really relearn you as *Georgia*. You'd feel idiotic, too, in making yourself self-important, as if you'd failed to grasp the essential impersonality of the name which isn't yours to alter, however dire your early days in the orphanage, and however impeccable your claim to rebaptism with that more glamorous name which, after all, you first were given.

You can hardly be accused of having fallen prey to a myth of your own origins, if originally you in fact *were* named *Georgia* or *Susquehanna* on your birth certificate and, having retrieved this document, you try to revert. Yet the supposition that really a myth of origins must be at work will triumph over the retrieved and factually historical name. For the stubborn fact is that without an established public ritual of renaming, the thing cannot be done. And any invented modern ritual would carry a synthetic and slightly foolish effect. But suppose you can't bear being called *Maureen* for another day, that your life creeps by unendurably bearing you headlong as *Maureen* to the grave? Murder is your only answer; you must drown her. Successful name-changing in a secular world would entail self-elimination — to present yourself from the outset to some utterly new cohort of acquaintance as *Georgia*, having severed yourself from the world in which you were *Maureen* by the classic device of leaving her clothes lying on the beach with a note. Short of this precarious melodrama, the awkwardness of trying to alter your given name isn't simply being caught out in your vanity, and imposing a laborious reminder on everyone else. There's more: it's as if the name changer has made a fundamental mistake about the nature of linguistic entitlement and has supposed that her own name *was* really hers to change. For a rough justice rules in the matter of calling others, indifferent to their own claims. We do not remotely care what our friends are called, just as long as they stay called it. And the effort of thinking of the *Boudicca* we've known for a quarter of a century as, from now onward, a *Gloriana* is all too much; some steps toward reclaiming one's birthright should never have been taken. In a culture which has no built-in rite of name changing to mark your accession to a finer stage of life, or to reflect an ancestral pedigree such as the elaborations of Igbo or Hausa customs, you will make yourself foolish. Or you will lay bare some past trauma as the reason for your change of given name, when this cause is, for everyone else, not linked to it; you will plunge your listeners into a strained faith or a piety of empathy in imagining your plight. As if you have made the mistake of taking too seriously something which, while officially intimately yours, does not matter to anyone else; for them it's an almost effaced mark, slim to the point of vanishing.

Isn't all this merely an unremarkable, if a mildly peculiar, side effect of given names? Of course we understand that they are *given*, we can't fail to grasp the fact that they were slapped onto us by somebody else, that as we grew we naturalized them, or we tried to, and we lived in them either pleasurably, or resentfully, or indifferently. Then surnames can also carry their histories of being roughly imposed, or refashioned in the name of tidiness, for instance, with the anglicizations of those who passed from central Europe through Ellis Island. But first-naming is a more distinctive example, through its pointedly sexed individuation, this name pinned to this body, of what happens routinely and quietly enough in life: the task of absorbing as your own something that you never chose. Once this phenomenon of becoming that which you are told you are is contemplated in relation to the usual attributes of your sex, your needs, your ethnicity, then in will rush all the associated politics, with their tendencies to exaggerate, to be it with a vengeance, to welcome it as a kind of arranged marriage in which affection may follow the contract, or to refuse or recast it as a social demand. Yet the impersonal benign tyranny of being stamped with an imposed personal name is such that it's harder to re-name yourself in particular than it is to become societally innovative in general.

Assuming this usual impossibility of a second adult christening, Stevenson mentions the hell endured by the bearers of "*punnable* names, names that stand alone, that have a significance and life apart from him that bears them. These are the bitterest of all. One friend of mine goes bowed and humbled through life under the weight of this misfortune; for it is an awful thing when a man's name is a joke, when he cannot be mentioned without exciting merriment, and when even the intimation of his death bids fair to carry laughter into many a home."[10] And yet, if well below the threshold of such gross misery, there's also a quite different and low-level endemic unease: the sheer unease of being called. Unthinkable as the alternative would be, there's something fundamentally embarrassing about possessing any name whatsoever. It's the being singled out. Then to articulate the name of one's beloved can be especially awkward. Kafka recorded this in his diary in 1912, shortly after his first meeting with his future love, Felice Bauer: "Thought a great deal about . . . what embarrassment at writing down names. . . . F.B."[11] But it's not simply the particular strain and shyness felt in articulating the delicate and momentous admission of *who* is loved. There's something else, something wider which inheres in naming: a sense of jarring. Incongruity springs from that odd and unsparing admixture of finiteness with arbitrariness, of the given with the contingent, which characterizes naming and being named. And where the unbounded aspirations of love meet the necessary restrictedness of the loved name, the impression is strong of something being nominally out of joint.

In this way the business of naming and being named offers a sharpened instance of the working of words in general, with its blend of capriciousness and authority, its sway over its users. There are, then, sound reasons for this impression of the faint but lingering absurdity of *being called* at all. Inhabiting the life of language means, too, that you just have to tolerate being accompanied by your own slight distance from your name. Yet here, as so often, a degree of "alienation" turns out to be a surprisingly better option than its implied alternative. Our nonalienation extracts the ultimate cost. For if our given names resemble luggage labels, at least the destination toward which they are traveling is democratically identical. Simple to imagine that to walk past your own first name and surname engraved on a tombstone, past the arrangement of these names identical to yours, perhaps of a long dead relative or perhaps of a complete stranger, would, after you'd made your first double take, compel you to dig your heels hard into the cemetery grass and gravel, firmly asserting your balance on this side of life. What you might next do is prove to yourself that you'd survived this apparent declaration of your own death by tracing, as in countless gothic movies, the chiseled incision of your name on the slab of the gravestone. But if this proof at your fingertips of your own survival were still to leave you in doubt, then your question to yourself of *"Was* I that name?" would not be perplexed, merely an idle musing which already understood its own unambiguous answer to be *yes*. For to be recorded as dead is the end of your nominal "alienation," and is the one point at which you do unequivocally rejoin your given name, to become it inalienably. Having no further use for it, it is only now that you can fully take it back from its givers.

*

NOTES

*

INTRODUCTION

1 Elias Canetti, "Word Attacks," in *The Conscience of Words*, trans. J. Neugroschel
   (New York: Seabury Press, 1979), 143.

2 Karl Marx, "The Eighteenth Brumaire of Louis Bonaparte," in *Collected Works
   of Karl Marx and Friedrich Engels*, vol. 11, 1851–53 (New York: International Publishers Company, 1979); *William James*, vol. 1, *The Principles of Psychology*, 2 vols.
   (New York: Henry Holt, 1890), 245–46; Heinrich von Kleist, "On the Gradual Production of Thoughts Whilst Speaking," in *Selected Writings*, ed. and
   trans. David Constantine (London: J. M. Dent, 1997), 405–9; Friedrich Nietzsche, *Beyond Good and Evil*, trans. R. J. Hollingdale (New York: Penguin Books,
   1973); Sigmund Freud, *The Standard Edition of the Complete Psychological Works
   of Sigmund Freud*, trans. James Strachey, vol. 8 (1905), *Jokes and their Relation to
   the Unconscious*, and vol. 14 (1917), *Mourning and Melancholia* (New York: W. W.
   Norton, 1990); Mikhail Bakhtin, "The Artist as Hero," in *Art and Answer-
   ability: Early Philosophical Essays*, ed. Michael Holquist and Vadim Liapunov,
   trans. Vadim Liapunov (Austin: University of Texas Press, 1990); Walter Benjamin, "On Language as Such and on the Language of Man" (1916), in *Walter
   Benjamin: Selected Writings*, vol. 1, 1913–1926, ed. Marcus Bullock and Michael
   W. Jennings (Cambridge: The Belknap Press of Harvard University Press,
   1996); Roman Jakobson, *Language in Literature*, ed. Krystyna Pomorska and
   Stephen Rudy (Cambridge: The Belknap Press of Harvard University Press,
   1987), 423; Martin Heidegger, *On the Way to Language*, trans. Peter Hertz
   (San Francisco, Calif.: HarperSanFrancisco, 1982) and his *Poetry, Language,
   Thought*, trans. Albert Hofstadter (New York: Harper and Row, 1975); Theo-
   dor Adorno, "On Lyric Poetry and Society," in *Notes to Literature*, vol. 1, trans.
   Shierry Weber Nicholsen (New York: Columbia University Press, 1991), 37–

54; William Empson, *Seven Types of Ambiguity* (London: Chatto and Windus, 1930); Ludwig Wittgenstein, *Philosophical Investigations*, trans. G. E. M. Anscombe (Oxford: Basil Blackwell, 1963), 166e; Jacques Lacan, *The Seminar of Jacques Lacan*, ed. Jacques-Alain Miller, trans. Sylvana Tomaselli (New York: W. W. Norton, 1988), book 2, 89–90; Michel Foucault, *Aesthetics, Method, and Epistemology*, vol. 2 of *The Essential Works of Michel Foucault, 1954–1984*, ed. James Faubion, trans. Robert Hurley (New York: New Press, 1999); Louis Althusser, *Lenin and Philosophy and Other Essays* (New York: Monthly Review Press, 2001); Samuel Beckett, "Texts for Nothing," in *Samuel Beckett: The Complete Short Prose 1929–1989*, ed. S. E. Gontarski (New York: Grove Press, 1995); Maurice Merleau-Ponty, *Phenomenology of Perception*, trans. Colin Smith (Atlantic Highlands, N.J.: Humanities Press, 1962), 177; Roland Barthes, *The Responsibility of Forms*, trans. Richard Howard (Berkeley: University of California Press, 1991), 269; Veronica Forrest-Thomson, *Poetic Artifice* (New York: St. Martin's Press, 1978); Gilles Deleuze and Félix Guattari, *A Thousand Plateaus: Capitalism and Schizophrenia*, trans. Brian Massumi (Minneapolis: University of Minnesota Press, 1987); Raymond Williams, *Marxism and Literature* (New York: Oxford University Press, 1977), 132; Douglas Oliver, *Poetry and Narrative in Performance* (London: Macmillan, 1989); Valentin Volosinov, *Marxism and the Philosophy of Language*, trans. Ladislav Matejka and I. R. Titunik (Cambridge, Mass.: Harvard University Press, 1973).

3 J. L. Austin, *How to Do Things with Words* (Cambridge, Mass.: Harvard University Press, 1975).

4 The argument of chapter 5 in Denise Riley, *The Words of Selves: Identification, Solidarity, Irony* (Stanford, Calif.: Stanford University Press, 2000).

5 See Denise Riley, " 'A Voice without a Mouth': Inner Speech," *Qui Parle* 14, no. 1 (2004).

ONE Malediction

1 See chapter 5 of my *The Words of Selves: Identification, Solidarity, Irony* (Stanford, Calif.: Stanford University Press, 2000).

2 Joan Scott, writing about history's phantasms, notes that "retrospective identifications, after all, are imagined repetitions and repetitions of imagined resemblances." "Fantasy Echo: History and the Construction of Identity," *Critical Inquiry* (winter 2001): 284–304 (quote, 287).

3 Riley, *The Words of Selves*, 84–89. For an introduction to the history of pragmatics, which does differently consider the forcefulness of language, see B. Nehrlich and D. Clarke, *Language, Action, Context: The Early History of Pragmatics in Europe and America, 1780–1930* (Amsterdam: John Benjamins, 1996).

4 The phenomenon of "audiation" and inner replaying is implicitly discussed in my chapter "A Voice without a Mouth," in *The Force of Language*, by Jean-Jacques Lecercle and Denise Riley (London: Palgrave Macmillan, 2004). (Audiation is the silent and private "running through the head" of music.)

5 This can be found, for instance, in some psychiatric classifications used in South America.

6 As Joan Scott writes, "the fantasy also implies a story about a sequential relationship for prohibition, fulfillment, and punishment (having broken the law that prohibits incest, the child is being beaten)." Scott, "Fantasy Echo," 290.

7 Jean Laplanche has remarked on the "message" which always comes to me from another, as an impingement on me of the other's unconscious, formative for my own, and has raised the question of how to take account of that constitutive alterity. "Confronted with this enigmatic message, a message compromised by any number of unconscious resurgences, the child translates it as best as he can, with the language at his disposal." Jean Laplanche, *Essays on Otherness*, ed. John Fletcher (New York: Routledge, 1998), 158–59.

8 A burden of his sustained discussion of pain and skepticism about its reporting, in his *Philosophical Investigations*, trans. G. E. M. Anscombe (Oxford: Basil Blackwell, 1963).

9 From "Adagia," in *Wallace Stevens: Collected Poetry and Prose*, ed. Frank Kermode and Joan Richardson (New York: Library of America, 1997), 907.

10 Jacques Lacan, "The Signification of the Phallus," in *Ecrits: A Selection*, trans. Alan Sheridan (London: Routledge, 2001), 315.

11 The Russian word *ideologiya* has, like *ideology*, debated meanings. As one glossary on Bakhtin's terms, by Graham Roberts, asserts, "The Russian ideologiya is less politically coloured than the English word 'ideology.' In other words, it is not necessarily a consciously held political belief system; rather it can refer in a more general sense to the way in which members of a given social group view the world. It is in this broader sense that Bakhtin uses the term. For Bakhtin, any utterance is shot through with 'ideologiya,' any speaker is automatically an ideologue." *The Bakhtin Reader*, ed. Pam Morris (London: Edward Arnold, 1994), 249.

12 V. N. Volosinov, *Marxism and the Philosophy of Language*, trans. from the 1930 edition by Ladislav Matejka and I. R. Titunik (New York and London: Seminar Press, 1973), 39.

13 Volosinov, *Marxism and the Philosophy of Language*, 29.

14 G. W. F. Hegel, *Phenomenology of Spirit*, trans. A. V. Miller (Oxford: Oxford University Press, 1977), 187.

15 Hegel, *Phenomenology of Spirit*, 188.

16 Jacques Lacan, "The Signification of the Phallus," 86–87.

17 ". . . through all the techniques of moral and human sciences that go to make up a knowledge of the subject." Gilles Deleuze, *Foucault*, trans. Sean Hand (London: Athlone Press, 1999), 103.

18 Hegel, *Phenomenology of Spirit*, 308.

19 Hegel, *Phenomenology of Spirit*, 116.

20 Marcus Aurelius, maxim 20, book 9, *Meditations*, trans. Maxwell Staniforth (London: Penguin Books, 1964), 142. See also, again in the spirit of Epictetus, his "That men of a certain type should behave as they do is inevitable. To wish it otherwise were to wish the fig tree would not yield its juice." Book 4, maxim 6, 65.

21 A recall of the title *Love's Work*, Gillian Rose (London: Chatto and Windus, 1995).

22 Hegel, *Phenomenology of Spirit*, 116.

23 "Just as the individual self-consciousness is immediately present in language, so it is also immediately present as a universal infection; the complete separation into independent selves is at the same time the fluidity and universally communicated unity of the many selves; language is the soul existing as soul." Ibid., 430.

24 Ibid., 119.

TWO "What I Want Back Is What I Was"

1 Epictetus, "The Handbook of Epictetus," in *The Discourses of Epictetus*, ed. Christopher Gill, rev. trans. by Robin Hard, Everyman series (London: J. M. Dent, 1995), 289.

2 And anyway we aren't innocent of what it does to us. We do things in return to it, through it. See the argument advanced throughout chapter 5 in my *The Words of Selves: Identification, Solidarity, Irony* (Stanford, Calif.: Stanford University Press, 2000).

3 William Shakespeare, Sonnet 77, discussed in Helen Vendler, *The Art of Shakespeare's Sonnets* (Cambridge, Mass.: The Belknap Press of Harvard University Press, 1997), 347.

4 "The Eye-Mote," in *Sylvia Plath: Collected Poems* (London: Faber and Faber, 1981), 109.

5 Maurice Merleau-Ponty, *The Primacy of Perception, and Other Essays*, trans. James. M. Edie (Evanston, Ill.: Northwestern University Press, 1964), 162–63.

6 In the movie *Death in Venice* (after Thomas Mann's 1912 novel) directed by Luchino Visconti, Italy, 1971.

7   G. W. F. Hegel, *The Introduction to Hegel's Philosophy of Fine Art*, trans. Bernard Bosanquet, Kegan Paul (London: Trench, Trubner and Co., 1905), 120.

8   Fran Lebowitz, *Metropolitan Life* (New York: E. P. Dutton, 1978), 6.

9   "The Lady's Dressing Room" (1732), in *Jonathan Swift: The Complete Poems*, ed. Pat Rogers (Harmondsworth, England: Penguin, 1983), 452.

10 Both men and women had facelifts in the early 1900s; Dr. Charles Miller's standard work of the period was *Cosmetic Surgery* (Philadelphia: F. A. Davis, 1907).

11 John Woodforde's *The History of Vanity* (Stroud: Alan Sutton, 1992), 22, which draws on Anthony Wallace's *The Progress of Plastic Surgery* (Oxford, 1982).

12 William Shakespeare, Sonnet 63, analyzed in Helen Vendler, *The Art of Shakespeare's Sonnets*, 295.

13 Shakespeare's Sonnet 12; see Vendler's discussion, ibid., 96.

14 Jonathan Swift, "When I Come to Be Old" (probably from 1699), in *The Prose Works of Jonathan Swift, D. D.*, vol. 1 (London: George Bell and Sons, 1897), xcii.

15 Denise Riley (written for this volume). The actual work of the lyricist Lorenz "Larry" Hart with the composer Richard Rodgers can be found in their many collaborations, such as the dark "Bewitched, Bothered and Bewildered," recorded by Ella Fitzgerald. Hart was the author of such fine lines as "In that mountain greenery / Where God paints the scenery."

16 "Ode on Melancholy" (c. 1820), in *John Keats: Selected Poems*, ed. Edmund Blunden (London: Collins, 1955), 269.

17 Epictetus, *The Discourses of Epictetus*, 315.

18 Boethius, born approximately 480 A.D., wrote,

>   Again, you think that you appear beautiful in many kinds of clothing. But if their form is pleasant to the eyes, I would admire the nature of the material or the skill of the maker. Out of all these possessions, then, which you reckon as your wealth, not one can really be shown to be your own. For if they have no beauty for you to acquire, what have they for which you should grieve if you lose them, or in keeping which you should rejoice? And if they are beautiful by their own nature, how are you the richer thereby?

>   *The Consolation of Philosophy*, trans. W. V. Cooper (London: J. M., London, 1902), 41–42.

19 Marcus Aurelius, *Meditations*, trans. Maxwell Staniforth (London: Penguin Books, 1964), 59.

20 Pierre Hadot, *Philosophy as a Way of Life*, ed. Arnold I. Davidson (Oxford: Blackwell, 1995), 209.

21 Ibid., 211.

22 His phrase is *toti se inserens mundo*. See ibid., 208.

23 Marcus Aurelius, *Meditations*, 67.

24 Epictetus, *The Discourses of Epictetus*, 281.

25 Ibid., 279.

26 Ibid., 280.

27 Ibid.

28 Michel Foucault, *The History of Sexuality*, vol. 3, *The Care of the Self*, trans. Robert Hurley (Harmondsworth, England: Penguin Books, 1990), 50.

29 Hadot, *Philosophy as a Way of Life*, 211.

30 Ibid., 211.

31 Foucault, *The Care of the Self*, 51.

32 "The Function and Field of Speech and Language in Psychoanalysis," in *Ecrits: A Selection*, trans. Alan Sheridan (London: Routledge, 1997), 94.

33 For a full explanation of this coinage, see my chapter "A Voice without a Mouth," in *The Force of Language*, by Jean-Jacques Lecercle and Denise Riley (Basingstoke, England: Palgrave Macmillan, 2004).

34 For instance, Jean Laplanche, Jean-Luc Nancy, and Philippe Lacoue-Labarthe.

35 Freud, "Infantile Material as a Source of Dreams," chapter 5 of *The Interpretation of Dreams*, trans. James Strachey, vol. 4 (Harmondsworth, England: Penguin Books, 1976), 295.

36 Cathy Caruth, "An Interview with Jean Laplanche," *Postmodern Culture: An Electronic Journal of Interdisciplinary Criticism* 11, no. 2 (January 2001), pars. 16 and 17.

37 "Affect, which is to say ambivalence, puts us at the heart of a sociality, of an 'unsociable sociality' as Kant's phrase would have it. At the heart, we will say, of a dis-sociation." Philippe Lacoue-Labarthe and Jean-Luc Nancy, "The Unconscious Is Destructured Like an Affect," *Stanford Literature Review* 6, no. 2 (fall 1989): 191–209 (quote, 201).

38 V. N. Volosinov, *Marxism and the Philosophy of Language*, translated from the 1930 edition by Ladislav Matejka and I. R. Titunik (New York: Seminar Press, 1973), 39. This point is argued at length in Jean-Jacques Lecercle and Denise Riley, *The Force of Language* (Basingstoke, England: Palgrave Macmillan, 2004).

39 Joan Scott, "Fantasy Echo: History and the Construction of Identity," *Critical Inquiry* 27 (winter 2001): 284–304 (quote, 292).

40 Hegel, *Phenomenology of Spirit*, trans. A. V. Miller (Oxford: Oxford University Press, 1977), 28.

41 An adaptation of Raymond Williams's phrase "structures of feeling," from his *Marxism and Literature* (Oxford: Oxford University Press, 1977), 132.

1 Behind this simple assertion lie generations of debate: "The word is a direct expression of the historical nature of human consciousness," as elaborated by L. S. Vygotsky, *Thought and Language*, ed. and trans. Eugenia Haufmann and Gertrude Vakar (Cambridge, Mass: MIT Press, 1986), 256.

2 The whole idea of a fraught transition from an emphatic innerness causes unhappiness in itself, according to Michel Henry, *The Genealogy of Psychoanalysis*, trans. Douglas Brick (Stanford, Calif.: Stanford University Press, 1993), 302.

3 Writing from the perspective of linguistic pragmatics, Mark Turner, "Figure," in *Figurative Language and Thought*, ed. N. Katz, C. Cacciari, R. W. Gibbs, and M. Turner (Oxford: Oxford University Press, 1998), 44–87 (quote, 63) suggests the example of the metaphor of intellectual progress as embodying a virtually literal sense of direction.

4 These, including Wolfson and Brisset, are discussed extensively and helpfully by Gérard Genette, *Mimologies*, trans. Thais E. Morgan (Lincoln: University of Nebraska Press, 1995), and by Jean-Jacques Lecercle, *The Violence of Language* (London: Routledge, 1990).

5 Michel Foucault, *Ethics: Subjectivity and Truth*, vol. 1 of *The Essential Works of Michel Foucault, 1954–1984*, ed. Paul Rabinow, trans. Robert Hurley et al. (London: Allen Lane, Penguin Press, 1997), 1:117, raises a possibility in his interview "Polemics, Politics, and Problematizations": "For a long time, I have been trying to see if it would be possible to describe the history of thought as distinct both from the history of ideas (by which I mean the analyses of systems of representation) and from the history of mentalities (by which I mean the analysis of attitudes and types of action)." Edward Casey's *The Fate of Place: A Philosophical History* (Los Angeles: University of California Press, 1997), gives an encyclopaedic description of metaphors of space within thought, yet doesn't dwell on the nature of this metaphoricity.

6 See the elaborations in Foucault, "The Thought of the Outside," in *Aesthetics, Method, and Epistemology*, vol. 2 of *Foucault, Essential Works*, ed. James D. Faubion, trans. Robert Hurley et al. (London: Allen Lane, Penguin Press, 1998), 2:147.

7 Or must the brain inevitably grasp its surrounding world as patterns of depths and surfaces? See the persuasive and highly readable neurological accounts in Antonio Damasio's study, *The Feeling of What Happens: Body and Emotion in the Making of Consciousness* (London: William Heinemann, 1999).

8 V. N. Volosinov, "Multiaccentuality and the Sign," *Marxism and the Philosophy*

of *Language*, trans. L. Matejka and I. R. Titunik (Cambridge, Mass: Harvard University Press, 1986), 9–24 (quote, 15).

9 It is vexed for linguists, too. So the metaphor of "I see" or "I grasp" for "I understand," where a systematic series of metaphors of visualizing or apprehension stand for comprehension, supports Eve Sweetser's contention that metaphoricity migrates from the outside to the inside. Sweetser, *From Etymology to Pragmatics: Metaphorical and Cultural Aspects of Semantic Structure* (Cambridge: Cambridge University Press, 1990). She observes, "Thus we could say that 'This fact blocks us from reaching that conclusion.' This is another manifestation of the same broader mapping of external selves onto internal selves, and the forces and barriers of our external world onto those of our internal world" (66).

10 Jacques Donzelot, *The Policing of Families*, preface to the English edition, trans. Robert Hurley (Baltimore: Johns Hopkins University Press, 1997), xxvii.

11 "Metaphysics has always thought sociality as either a positive election, a reciprocal esteem of subjects, or as the coercion of a pure force." Philippe Lacoue-Labarthe and Jean-Luc Nancy, "The Unconscious Is Destructured Like an Affect," *Stanford Literature Review* 6, no. 2 (fall 1989): 191–209 (quote, 207).

12 See Maurice Merleau-Ponty's meditations here, especially "Nothing determines me from outside, not because nothing acts upon me, but, on the contrary, because I am from the start outside myself and open to the world." Merleau-Ponty, *Phenomenology of Perception*, trans. Colin Smith (London: Routledge and Kegan Paul, 1978), 456.

13 But enunciation also has a long history as a concept. See, for instance, Todorov's *L'énonciation* (Paris: Didier Larousse, 1970). In aspects of Foucault's work, and especially with Gilles Deleuze and Félix Guattari, *A Thousand Plateaus*, trans. Brian Massumi (London: Athlone Press, 1990), 75–110, "bodies" are whatever thing or condition can act or be acted on, and "enunciations" are any incorporeal but effective transforming statements which act on and through them.

14 Gaston Bachelard, *The Poetics of Space*, trans. Maria Jolas (Boston: Beacon Press, 1969), 215.

15 G. W. E. Russell, *Collections and Recollections, By One Who Has Kept a Diary* (London: 1898), 182.

16 Like the idea of the "fold of the self" that Deleuze discusses apropos Foucault, in his *Foucault*, trans. Sean Hand (London: Athlone, 1988), 94–123. Or Philippe Lacoue-Labarthe and Jean-Luc Nancy, "The Unconscious Is Destructured Like an Affect," 198: "For the affect, if it is, is only that: the affec-

tion of an inside by the outside, therefore the division of the two *and* their [*reciprocal* penetration. Ambivalence is thus the affect itself, that is to say, the oscillation of what one] could call an excision occurring as an incision (which would be completely different from a castration), the incisive excision out of which arises a subject (or at least its project). And consequently— since this subject departs itself as well—an object."

17 Bachelard, *The Poetics of Space*, 222.

18 G. W. F. Hegel, *Phenomenology of Spirit*, trans. A. V. Miller (Oxford and New York: Oxford University Press, 1977), 174.

19 By his mention of this standing of the family as the cult of the dead in his "Analysis of the Text," J. N. Findlay no doubt intended a scholarly observation, not the acerbic aside we might imagine. Findlay, "Analysis of the Text," in Hegel, *Phenomenology of the Spirit*, trans. A. V. Miller (Oxford: Oxford University Press, 1977), 495–591 (quote, 552).

20 The English poet and cleric, in his (unpaginated) *Devotions of 1624*, reprinted as *Devotions upon Emergent Occasions, [and] Death's Duel* (Ann Arbor: University of Michigan Press, 1985), 17.

21 Lacoue-Labarthe and Nancy, "The Unconscious Is Destructured Like an Affect," 119.

22 " 'Others' is the inordinate measure of an outside which affects from within, of an inside which affects itself on the outside—or of an alterity which increases with its sameness, a sameness which grows with its affectivity. Affect, which is to say ambivalence, puts us at the heart of a sociality, of an 'unsociable sociality' as Kant's phrase would have it. At the heart, we will say, of a dis-sociation." Lacoue-Labarthe and Nancy, "The Unconscious Is Destructured Like an Affect," 191.

23 Virginia Woolf, *To The Lighthouse* (London: Hogarth Press, 1927), 114.

24 Exodus 20:17.

25 Sheepish, I mean, following Theodor Adorno, *Hegel: Three Studies*, trans. Shierry Weber Nicholsen (Cambridge, Mass.: MIT Press, 1993), 194, who warns against the authoritarian impulse lurking behind any utterance of the form "Speaking as a something-or-other, I." "Transcendent critique sympathises with authority in its very form, even before expressing any content: there is a moment of content to the form itself. The expression 'as a . . . , I . . . ,' in which one can insert any orientation, from dialectical materialism to Protestantism, is symptomatic of that."

26 Moustapha Safouan, personal communication, 2001.

27 So alarmed debates in the House of Lords in London have recently asked whether the implication of the proclaimed advantage for any child in having

two parents, not just one, was that two "stable" homosexual parents might be just as good as two heterosexual parents.

28 A line spoken by the late actor Raul Julia, in the movie *Addams Family Values 2*, directed by Barry Sonnenfeld, screenplay by Paul Rudnick (Paramount Pictures, 1993).

29 As with ancient forms: up to the seventeenth century, the family was originally a word for the social association within a household, and not a blood tie. See Raymond Williams, *Keywords* (London: Fontana, 1981), 131.

30 See the implications inherent in Jane Lewis's study. Jane Lewis, ed. *Lone Mothers in European Welfare Regimes* (London: Jessica Kingsley Publishers, 1997). Also, Carolyn Wright and Gill Jagger, eds. *Changing Family Values* (London: Routledge, 1999), 180, criticize the frequent use of data which obscures the specific states of single parent families, and ask how much newer and more refined definitions have entered into recent sociology.

31 P. N. Furbank, *Diderot: A Critical Biography* (New York: Martin Secker and Warburg, 1992), 151. My thanks to Susan Clarke for this.

FOUR Some WHYs and *why mes*

1 King James Authorized Version of the Bible, Job 3:11.

2 Job 8:2.

3 Aron Ronald Bodenheimer, *Warum? Von der Obszönität des Fragens* (Stuttgart: Reclam, 1999).

4 George Eliot, *Middlemarch* (New York: Modern Library), 846.

5 Jacques Lacan, "The Function and Field of Speech and Language in Psychoanalysis," in *Ecrits: A Selection*, trans. Alan Sheridan (London: Routledge, 2001), 94.

6 Michel de Montaigne, *Essais 1580–1595*, book 1, chapter 27, "De l'Amitié," ed. P. Michel (Paris: Folio, Gallimard, 1982), 269. The quotation means, "Because it's him, because it's me."

7 Roland Barthes, *A Lover's Discourse*, in *A Barthes Reader*, ed. Susan Sontag (New York: Noonday Press, 1983), 431.

8 See Judith Butler, *Excitable Speech: A Politics of the Performative* (London: Routledge, 1997) and also her *The Psychic Life of Power: Theories in Subjection* (Stanford, Calif.: Stanford University Press, 1997).

9 G. W. F. Hegel, *Phenomenology of Spirit*, trans. A. V. Miller (Oxford: Oxford University Press, 1977), 407.

10 July 1917, "On Slogans," in V. I. Lenin, *Collected Works*, vol. 25 (London: Lawrence and Wishart, 1964), 185. See the discussion of this in Jean-Jacques Lecercle, *The Violence of Language* (London: Routledge, 1990), 209–12.

11 This is argued throughout chapter 5 of my *The Words of Selves: Identification, Solidarity, Irony* (Stanford, Calif.: Stanford University Press, 2000).

12 Ludwig Wittgenstein, *Philosophical Investigations*, trans. G. E. M. Anscombe (Oxford: Basil Blackwell, 1963), par. 655, 167e.

FIVE Linguistic Inhibition

1 My *The Words of Selves: Identification, Solidarity, Irony* (Stanford, Calif.: Stanford University Press, 2000), 56–92, has a long discussion about what linguistic unease is.

2 William James, *The Principles of Psychology*, vol. 1 (London: Macmillan, 1890), 281.

3 See Keith Allan and Kate Burridge, *Euphemism and Dysphemism: Language Used as Shield and Weapon* (New York: Oxford University Press, 1991).

4 The drawback of the study of the single word as such is described by Deleuze and Guattari: "As long as linguistics confines itself to constants, whether syntactical, morphological, or phonological, it ties the statement to a signifier and enunciation to a subject and accordingly botches the assemblage; it consigns circumstances to the exterior, closes language in on itself, and makes pragmatics a residue." Gilles Deleuze and Félix Guattari, *A Thousand Plateaus: Capitalism and Schizophrenia*, trans. Brian Massumi (London: Athlone Press, 1988), 82.

5 See Stanley Cavell, "The Avoidance of Love: A Reading of King Lear," in *Must We Mean What We Say?* (Cambridge: Cambridge University Press, 2002), 267–353.

6 William Shakespeare, *King Lear*, 1.1.87–91, in *The Norton Shakespeare*, ed. Stephen Greenblatt, Walter Cohen, Jean E. Howard, and Katharine Eisaman Maus (New York: W. W. Norton, 1997), 2322.

7   We know what happens next: the young woman leaves her hand there, but she does not notice that she is leaving it. She does not notice because it happens by chance that she is at this moment all intellect. She draws her companion up to the most lofty regions of sentimental speculation; she speaks of Life, of her life, she shows herself in her essential aspect—a personality, a consciousness. And during this time the divorce of the body from the soul is accomplished; the hand rests inert between the warm hands of her companion— neither consenting nor resisting—a thing.

Jean-Paul Sartre, *Being and Nothingness*, trans. Hazel E. Barnes (New York: Washington Square Press, 1966), 101.

8 George Eliot, *Middlemarch* (New York: Modern Library, 1992), chapter 80,

846. This passage is also discussed in chapter 4, "Some WHYs and *why mes*," here.

9 It's partly an effect of the history of contraceptive techniques and the availability of abortion. At times men, too, would have dreaded an unwanted pregnancy; their taking some responsibility to avoid it could but need not imply altruism—rather a dread of getting saddled.

10 See Robert J. Stanton and Gore Vidal, eds., *Views from a Window: Conversations with Gore Vidal* (New York: Lyle Stuart, 1980), 239.

11 This figures in Heinrich Himmler's version of linguistic delicacy:

> I want to also mention a very difficult subject before you, with complete candour. It should be discussed amongst us, yet nevertheless, we will never speak about it in public. Just as we did not hesitate on June 30 to carry out our duty as ordered, and stand comrades who had failed against the wall and shoot them—about which we have never spoken, and never will speak. That was, thank God, a kind of tact natural to us, a foregone conclusion of that tact, that we have never conversed about it amongst ourselves, never spoken about it, everyone shuddered, and everyone was clear that the next time, he would do the same thing again, if it were commanded and necessary. I am talking about the evacuation of the Jews, the extermination of the Jewish people.

From Himmler's speech at Posen, October 4, 1943, as transcribed by the Nizkor Project, http://www.nizkor.org/hweb/people/h/himmler-heinrich/.

12 "There is violence involved in the linguistic struggle for places, ie in the linguistic process of subjectivation." Jean-Jacques Lecercle, *The Violence of Language* (London: Routledge, 1990), 257.

SIX "Lying" When You Aren't

1 "Je suis un mensonge qui dit toujours la vérité." Quoted in "Opéra: Le paquet rouge," in *Jean Cocteau, Oeuvres poétiques 1925–1927* (Paris: Librairie Stock, 1927).

2 *Hamlet*, 3:2, *The Norton Shakespeare*, ed. Stephen Greenblatt, Walter Cohen, Jean E. Howard, and Katharine Eisaman Maus (New York: W. W. Norton, 1997), p. 1713.

3 Sigmund Freud, "Some Character Types Met with in Psycho-analytic Work: Criminals from a Sense of Guilt," in *The Standard Edition of the Complete Psychological Works of Sigmund Freud*, trans. James Strachey, vol. 14 (1917) (London: Hogarth Press, 1964), 332–33.

4 Alexis de Tocqueville, *Recollections: The French Revolution of 1848* (New Brunswick, N.J.: Transaction Books, 1990), 4.

5 Bertrand Russell, *The Autobiography of Bertrand Russell*, vol. 1 (London: George Allen and Unwin, 1967), 64.

6 H. L. Mencken, *A Mencken Chrestomathy* (New York: Random House, 1949), 617.

7 John Forrester writes on just this point, "The formulation 'my parents know my thoughts' is the formulation of speech—all of thought is to be found in the Other (the discourse of the Other)." But then, as Forrester continues, Lacan points out that later you discover this is not true—as the capacity to lie makes evident. John Forrester, *Truth Games: Lies, Money and Psychoanalysis* (Cambridge, Mass.: Harvard University Press, 2000), 98.

8 François Duc de La Rochefoucauld, Maxim 84, in *Reflections: Or Sentences and Moral Maxims*, trans. Leonard Tancock (Harmondsworth: Penguin, 1959), 45.

9 Stendhal, *Love*, trans. Gilbert and Suzanne Sale (London: Merlin Press, 1957), 92.

EIGHT "But Then I Wouldn't Be Here"

1 Sigmund Freud, "Jokes and Their Relation to the Unconscious" (1905), *Standard Edition of the Complete Psychological Works of Sigmund Freud*, ed. James Strachey, vol. 8 (London: Hogarth Press, 1964), 57.

2 See Randall Kennedy, *Nigger—The Strange Career of a Troublesome Word* (New York: Vintage Books, 2003).

3 "Transcendent critique sympathises with authority in its very form, even before expressing any content: there is a moment of content to the form itself. The expression 'as a . . . , I . . . ,' in which one can insert any orientation, from dialectical materialism to Protestantism, is symptomatic of that." Theodor Adorno, *Hegel: Three Studies*, trans. Shierry Weber Nicholsen (Cambridge, Mass.: MIT Press, 1993), 194.

4 Wendy Brown, *States of Injury* (Princeton, N.J.: Princeton University Press, 1995), 75–76.

5 *Monty Python's Life of Brian*, directed by Terry Jones. Python [Monty] Pictures Ltd., UK, 1979.

NINE Your Name Which Isn't Yours

1 Gertrude Stein, *Lectures in America* (New York: Random House, 1935), 210.

2 Pamela Samuelson, *Baby Names for the New Century* (New York: Harpertorch, Harper Mass Market Paperback, 1994).

3 This is the argument of Stanley Lieberson in *A Matter of Taste: How Names, Fashions, and Culture Change* (New Haven, Conn.: Yale University Press, 2000).

time I wrote this, *Chloe* has been dethroned. See United Kingdom
✓ of National Statistics, 6 January 2003, http://www.statistics.gov.uk/
ₛpecials/babiesnames_girls.asp.

5 Robert Louis Stevenson, "The Philosophy of Nomenclature," in *Lay Morals* (London: Chatto and Windus, 1911), 161.

6 Denise Riley, *The Words of Selves: Identification, Solidarity, Irony* (Stanford, Calif.: Stanford University Press, 2000), 158.

7 John Stuart Mill, *A System of Logic* (London: Longmans, 1961), 20.

8 Stevenson, *Lay Morals*, 158.

9 Tannette Johnson-Elie, *Milwaukee Journal Sentinel, JS Online*, 5 February 2003, http://www.jsonline.com/bym.

10 Stevenson, *Lay Morals*, 160.

11 *The Diaries of Franz Kafka*, edited by Max Brod. See Kafka's diary entry for 15 August 1912 (New York: Schocken Books 1948), 267.

Denise Riley is a Professor in the Faculty of Arts
and Humanities at the University of East Anglia.
Her books include *"Am I That Name?": Feminism and
the Category of "Women" in History* and *The Words of
Selves: Identification, Solidarity, Irony.*

*

Library of Congress Cataloging-in-
Publication Data
Riley, Denise
Impersonal passion : language as affect /
Denise Riley.
p. cm.
Includes bibliographical references and index.
ISBN 0-8223-3500-X (hardcover : alk. paper)
ISBN 0-8223-3512-3 (pbk. : alk. paper)
1. Language and emotions.   2. Psycholinguistics.
I. Title.
P37.R54 2005
401'.9—dc22   2004018748